Tracey's Secret

David Arthur Walters

Published by David Arthur Walters, 2024.

TRACEY'S SECRET

First edition. November 21, 2024.

ISBN: 979-8230299400

Written by David Arthur Walters.

Table of Contents

Tracey's South Beach Suicide

I certainly understand why my next door neighbor, Tracey Flagler, may she rest in peace, opted out of her conditioned life in South Beach on Thanksgiving Day of 2007. I nearly did the same thing myself one New Year's Day, so I have no right to blame her. Besides, what person in her right mind would want to live forever in the very world of circumstances that had made her so miserable? In any event, many reasons can be found for committing suicide.

Tracey had high expectations, and wherever expectations run high, disappointments are accordingly severe. In any event, there is no end to desire. The bare necessities are never enough, and wants are multiplied with the supplies as advertised. Tracey Flagler had food, clothing, shelter and a bicycle, but that was not enough: she went to the movies, she watched television, she read magazines, and she served rich and famous people at the restaurant, observing them having a lot of fun, and she read prophets who said the purpose of life is to have fun, and Oprah agreed with them, and Tracey wanted more than what she had, and she didn't get it, and the prophets said there was no such thing as death, and she apparently threw away everything she had along with the slim chance that everyone is supposed to have in this great nation of ours, the chance to get filthy rich.

Tracey tried very hard to appreciate the quality of her life, which was no doubt better than that of untold millions of inhabitants of this planet, and the fact that she tried so hard makes it evident that it was not for her in the first place. She was young and attractive and passionate, a fun-loving girlfriend to her boyfriends; she was always able to find good jobs serving delicious food; she picked up hundreds of dollars in tips almost whenever she wanted to; she had a modest studio two blocks from a beautiful beach. But none of that was enough. She suffered terribly for the dearth of some ineluctable thing that she thought was the purpose and point of life, namely fun or joy. She never had enough fun, and thought the lack was due to a shortage of stuff. The pop prophets reinforced her faith in fun and in the notion that it can be purchased. Her notebooks reiterate endlessly the impoverished terminology of the instant success cult: I, want, fun, joy, me, feel, source, Oprah, money, stuff, famous, Madonna, eternal, rich, universe, attraction, vibrations.... And then there are the almost pathological perseverations, the fearful chanting of positive affirmations – unfortunately, we cannot make ourselves appreciate something simply by affirming the appreciation that we don't really have over and over again.

The handwritten menus and lists of ingredients in various dishes that I found in Tracey's notebooks are far more mouthwatering, and led me to believe that her life would have been richer if she had focused her intensely passionate nature on the objective details of things, on the consideration of other people, on the study of some liberal art she might have some interest in – a course in academic philosophy might have disenchanted her of the popular delusions.

At the bottom of Tracey's being there was an awful want, a terrible desire, a craving so intense that only a Buddha or a withdrawing drug addict could fathom it. Of course the inchoate desire she suffered was not unique. We have it in common, but we manage to cover it up, put it on a leash, subdue it, repress it, ignore it, or just accept it and suffer it. Some suffer it more than others, and poor Tracey simply could not tolerate the suffering. She wanted to believe the hype that the purpose of life is a constant joy that can be had in hand, instead of admitting the truth, that human nature is suffering, and that without it even fleeting joy would be impossible. She had her doubts about the eternal joy business: she expressed her anger at the false prophets in writing from time to time: "I HATE you, I HATE all of you!"

That is not to say that overt suffering is a good thing or that we should suffer needlessly. Freud was right: Neurotic people cling to their misery in self-defense no matter what paradise is promised. Sometimes we suffer only because we want to, although we don't know it. I developed a habit of asking myself, when miserable, "Do I want to make myself miserable?" No? Then I dwell on something else, and that's the end of that. Thoughts do influence matter, that much is self-evident, but the magic of positive thinking needs the right means.

Tracey thought a million dollars would afford her more leisure to have the kind of fun she wanted to have. Most of us without a million bucks would not mind having a million or more. If only everyone could get their hands on a million dollars our world would presumably be a much better place to live in, provided inflation could be held to less than two percent per annum.

Yes, a million dollars would make room for more fun, but fun at doing what? If I had a million dollars I might quit my day job tomorrow and invest my time in saving the world with success books. Ideally they would be written, edited and published by Yours Truly under my Three Stooges Publishing imprimatur

I already have the first book in mind, *How to Make a Million Dollars for Somebody Else*. I shall submit it for approval by Oprah Winfrey's book club. I can see myself now, chatting with Oprah on her show, explaining how the world would be a much better place if everyone would try to make a million dollars for someone else rather than for themselves, and I shall suggest that she use some of her $2.5 billion to sponsor a brand new reality show called *The Pot Latchers*. I shall bring along Tracey's One Million Dollar Bill coffee mug and some her catnip tea for people who like to see magic stuff, and I shall bring along Penelope, her teddy bear, too. Tracey loved cats, so ten percent of the profits would go into the Tracey Flagler Foundation for Stray Cats.

Oh, Dear Tracey, I did not know you when you were here, but I know you well enough now, and I miss you. You were welcome here. You thought you were a weirdo; you thought that you did not fit in here because your craving was not satisfied; you felt nobody could make you whole or fill your hole. If only you had known that South Beach is for weirdos, and that you would have fit right in here. We could have had fun suffering life together. We could have had fun riding in limos. We would have gotten on the Oprah show. We would have opened up an erotica boutique, a tattoo parlor, and a night club on Washington Avenue. Yes, we would have suffered, but we would have had a great deal of fun even if that is not the purpose of life.

All Hail Shaloma!

Tracey Flagler was a New Age woman through and through. She had become acquainted with The Source while working as waitress in South Beach, Her main ambition was to become a medium and high priestess of the postmodern cult. That was made clear in the diaries I recovered from her apartment after her tragic suicide. Therein I found nine tenets from one of the several entities she channeled:

-1-

Rejoice! The Ultimate Reality and Purpose of YOUR Eternal Life is Bliss, YOUR feeling of Absolute Joy. Have Fun, O Dear One! YOU are a Feeling Being. YOU are what YOU feel. YOUR feelings changes things. YOUR feelings transform objects as YOU perceive them. Therefore Elate YOURSELF, save the World that is YOU! Cheer Up, O Dear One! YOUR Joy recreates the objects YOU were formerly depressed about, into the Very Substance of Joy. YOUR Mission is to experience Joy and to Have Fun at all times. Rejoice!

-2-

Rejoice! The Inner Higher SELF is the Source of the Joy that YOU connect with, evolve toward, and become at-one with through SELF-realization. YOUR SELF itSELF is God by Virtue of Identification. But YOUR SELF does not lose its In-Dividuality and perish when it becomes One with the All, for the All is YOUR Multidimensional SELF comprising Infinite Possibilities, each being realized somewhere in Consciousness, no matter how minutely. In effect, the Potency for which YOUR human-potential strives is Omnipotence, and in this Absolute Freedom YOUR SELF enjoys Unimpeded Being. Rejoice

-3-

Rejoice! God is Infinite and is and is not everything at once. Take Heart! YOU, the SELF-God, are Like-Wise Unlimited. Be Gladdened, O Dear One. The SELF-God would persevere forever without impediment if it could, and in fact it can and it does so in YOU, an Ideally Instantiated Fact that the evolving YOU becomes fully Self-Aware of in Eternity. Rejoice!

-4-

Rejoice! It follows that the SELF is Immortal, that YOU cannot die, and that the apparent death and dissolution of the human body is not the death of YOUR True Form or Soul or SELF, which may choose to create, take on and cast off another form at will. Rejoice! -5- Rejoice! Since God is the Omnipotent, SELF-Created, SELF-Moved, First Mover who creates Reality by merely thinking it in terms of the Word created for that Purpose, the SELF-God creates its own Reality including its SELF by chanting the Word. Everything thus thoughtfully created is a Mode of Consciousness although, apparently, largely unconscious. The so-called Unconscious is not really Unconscious-In-ItSELF: it is Profoundly and Unutterably Conscious, and holds sway over Conscious-Consciousness; this Fun-Loving Merry Mind is the Source of God's Marvelous Mysteries, and should be exalted accordingly. Rejoice!

-6-

Rejoice! Since the SELF's Word becomes the SELF-Chosen Material World, all wishes come true, and the truly SELF-realized SELF has no desire to reject the World and become Homeless or Other-Worldly. The SELF-Created World belongs to the SELF; however, the SELF does not exactly own the World: the World is precisely the Derivative World of YOUR Choices. Enjoy Your Profit O

Dear One! God is of course Opulent; the World is Her bauble; hence the SELF-Realized SELF or YOU does not eschew riches but embraces them, adorns Her-SELF with them, and chants the Exhilarating Gospel of Wealth. Rejoice!

-7-

Rejoice! Until its Atonement, the In-Dividual, divided against its SELF by ignorance of its SELF, must endeavor to have Fun for its Own Salvation or SELF-Unity, and since its Own SELF is the SELF-God within every One, within each and every Member of the Category of One, Global Salvation may be accelerated if the SELF so chooses, by giving Profitable Service to Humanity, but that Service is Insufficient, for ultimately only SELF-Service Saves. Be Gay, O Dear One! Rejoice!

-8-

Rejoice! The SELF-God is ultimately responsible to YOU: Every One gets what S/HE deserves, for S/HE has in one way or another chosen those just deserts. The SELF shall evolve accordingly, from form to form, until full awareness of its Divinity-in-Unity is achieved. All who embrace the Future and take responsibility for their own SELF shall in the End eternally dwell in Joy-Full Harmony in the Peaceful Sphere. Therefore Exalt YOUR SELF, O Gleeful One! The Instantiated State of Ideal Peace is beyond good and evil; all goods and evils along the way are relative; since Divine Selves seek the same End, namely Good, there is no such thing as sin. Rejoice!

-9-

Everything God does, including what ignorance foolishly perceives to be evil, is really Good – there is no such thing as evil: God does not need a devil to be God. What is true of God is true of the virtually identical SELF that is YOU. In any event, no matter what is done, Good Intentions shall suffice to sanction the deed! Rejoice!

Tracey's South Beach Neighborhood

Tracey Flagler, may she rest in peace, was my neighbor. I barely knew her when she was with us, but after I found her remains in her apartment, I thought she might be any one of us despite our differences. The soul is bared when the body is decomposed, a soul essentially simple, without height, breadth or depth, at once boundless, numberless, and one. Reality when beheld from the right angle is an inexhaustible diamond mine no matter where an author might dig. Now that Tracey is gone for good, she is quintessentially as good a subject as her great idol, Oprah Winfrey, who was in Africa when she needed her, and who no doubt would have come to her rescue if only she had known of her desperate plight.

A ragged servant and a rich queen in this great log-cabin to white-house or squalid ghetto apartment to $50 million mansion nation of ours are at most and at least born equal, and to that equality all are fated to return. Notwithstanding a final judgment on their accidental particulars as individuals, they are hypothetically not only categorically the same as an existential category of one, but are in the final analysis are substantially the same as well. Although only individuals may apparently exist; although there may be no substantial continuity between individual things; although there may be no universals binding particulars; although the forms we perceive may be illusory, accidental configurations of matter; - still, in order to maintain our dignity, a wondrous exception must be made for our divine soul.

Undoubtedly that soul is not merely a name for Nothing or the Vanity of vanities: no, it is not an empty excuse for nothing but ignorance, but it is rather the supreme personal being, the universal I-god who presides over the cosmic stuff. Withal, no man in his right mind is a nominalist in his own right.

Tracey was virtually alone in this crowded world. She had no known heirs, and the personal effects that survived her were seemingly too inconsiderable to make an estate of any interest to the state. In any event, the stuff in her apartment was up for grabs, thanks to our landlord – he left her door open before the Salvation Army truck arrived. My fellow neighbors carted off a few of her things, but they missed what I discovered in the proverbial Field of Diamonds, that is to say, one's own backyard. The hidden treasure was worth more than the million dollars Tracey had asked the Source for in Oprah's name, money she needed to relax and have fun, to be free to be joyful every minute, free to be the proud proof of the success everyone wants, instead of scraping out a meager living as a hassled waitress for tourists and the occasional rich and famous people whom she wanted to join at table instead of wait at table.

Although she wanted more than what she had, Tracey very much enjoyed her South Beach apartment. She left notes behind expressing her appreciation.

"I am glad to have a city and a place to live in and my health and my kitties – I'm glad to have that in my life. Success is based on enjoying and appreciating physical stuff. I begin by appreciating the stuff I already have. I appreciate South Beach and the beautiful ocean, the colors and the architecture of South Beach. I appreciate the beautiful things in my apartment: my TV, my overstuffed chair, my kitties, all of the cool colors, my plastic glasses, my Etch 'O Sketch, my dry-eraser board. Yes, it is small compared to the mega-stuff I have asked for, and I feel stupid, but it is so BIG compared to what I once had. I am angry that I allowed myself to dream so big, yet I can harbor so much more in JOY than I used to be able to. Is there any reason that I can't continue? Why cannot I continue to keep up my success?"

The apartment Tracey appreciated so much is in a small complex on one of the last half-dozen blocks of the blighted old South Beach ghetto that has otherwise been gentrified. It is barely a stone's throw from the so-called chic scene on the southern extremity of the City of Miami Beach, the living end dubbed 'South Beach' by the promoters, where Tracey worked as a waitress, and is a mere block from Washington Avenue, the vulgar, drug-ridden nightclub strip favored by tattooed hip-hoppers and mentally ill vagrants. The rental property has an assessed value of one-million dollars and comprises three small two-story buildings, four identical studio apartments to each building, squeezed into a perpendicular row from street to alley. Living quarters therein are dirt cheap: $750 per month; the equivalent of the first and last month's rent must be deposited in advance as security.

A severely damaged sculpture, a tall monolithic wooden structure onto which an illusory resemblance of the face of Mona Lisa was slashed with a saw, stands out front in a small plaza. The sculptor sprayed it with graffiti and smashed the face of his creation before he moved out. The landlord, who complains that he has little money for maintenance because his rental profit has been taxed out of existence, has not bothered to remove it. The plaza out front as well as the narrow yard and sidewalks all around the buildings are usually cluttered with trash, socks, rags and underpants tossed out of the windows next door, dead palm leaves, sticky palm nuts, motor scooters, and dog excrement – as we say, "It's the culture, stupid."

A five-foot high, white metal picket fence runs along three sides of the property. The fence is for naught since the tenants could care less about keeping the gates locked, or are afraid to lock them: a resident was stabbed into a comatose state by a homeless man who was angered at him for locking them, thus denying him a convenient easement from the alley to the street. Club-goers drop by occasionally and use the premises as a toilet, as do the huge dogs that live on the premises – the place has been likened to a kennel. One resident dog lover recently had to move out of his apartment in our complex and off the beach because it is illegal to keep pit bulls on Miami Beach. His pit bull-Doberman mongrel was over-friendly yet presented a terrifying aspect as it played, tearing around corners of our buildings lickety-split to charge at any two-legged prospective playmate in sight. The dog's master, a waiter at a popular restaurant nearby, was a nice enough fellow, but his culture mandated shouting commands interspersed with key curse words at the dog at all hours of night, not cleaning up after the dog, and yelling Ebonics into his cell phone while pacing outside our windows when he got angry, using frightful gangster-rap talk.

When nature calls, animals respond. The sound of two ladies simultaneously talking on their cell phones woke me up late one night last week. With miniskirts pulled up and panties around ankles; they were urinating underneath Tracey's stairwell, just below her neighbor's window downstairs. I put the finely rounded brown asses of the two squatting ladies in the spotlight with my flashlight; they squealed, pulled up their panties in a hurry and scurried away. And late last evening, a couple came onto the property and took shelter from the rain under Tracey's stairwell. Their groaning sounds awoke me, and I thought someone was hurting. I went to the window; the couple was obviously having consensual sex, so I retired to let them have their way. Of course some of the hundreds of vagrants who live in South Beach alleys sometimes sleep on our outside stairwells. And one homeless man regularly uses the outside electrical outlet to charge his cell phone late at night – if only he would not talk on it so loudly, nobody would know.

The large abutting building walling off the north side of our ground is a hotel residence occupied by non-English speaking Hispanics, the majority of them illegal aliens. The shrinking economy is sending some of them back to impoverished Mexico as I write. They are a relatively peaceful lot. One was dumping his garbage onto our six-foot wide lawn along the building, but we found his phone number on a takeout slip for tacos in the garbage – a phone call threatening to call the police and immigration resolved the problem immediately. Two large-bodied workers who place their shoes and socks on the window sill can be seen sleeping in one small bed from time to time. Another tenant therein plays raucous Mexican music for an hour each evening. In case anyone is interested in such details, the inhabitants without curtains may be viewed taking showers.

Lawrence, a next door neighbor, mentioned Tracey shortly after I moved into my second-floor studio in the building in front of hers – I could look directly into her place from my back window in the bathroom. He said she was a sweet girl, and that if he were straight he would definitely go for her, but he doubted he would get very far because, he said, she preferred black men, an assumption made from a handsome brown gentleman regularly seen at her door – why do we whites have to work so hard for our tans? Lawrence, a New Yorker through and through, apparently had no such color preferences. He said he had overheard Teddy, our Puerto Rican neighbor downstairs, making racist remarks on his cell phone; he said was deeply offended by such low-class talk, although he was otherwise impressed by Freddy's linguistic facility, particularly his elocution and smooth tone of voice.

I did not think it was so smooth: Teddy did not want to disturb his own family, so he was wont to come outside and yell into his cell phone below our windows. And then he liked to party with friends and a jug of wine on our stairwell. I spoke to him quietly about the annoyance, but he said he was the de facto resident manager; he said he did not care what I thought, that I should just move. I became the jerk who straightened him out the next night with a scene that included cops in the cast. He apologized through the landlord, and became quite the gentleman thereafter. He is now the head of a family of five including the dog, intimately cooped up in one room with a large entertainment center that thumps into the night until I call him or bang on his ceiling. He does try to be considerate, but our floors and walls are paper thin and he loves drumming. And now he takes his cell phone to the street for long calls. He could be a very successful family man, a man with a house and loving family and a backyard for the dog, if only he would reach for the stars. But he reached for Section 8 housing, and turned it down after waiting 3 years. He did not want to raise his kids in a violent ghetto so here he remains with a brand new baby. I want him to be successful, but my own circumstances are certainly not a pulpit from which normal success can be preached without hypocrisy – I am presently a successful failure.

Lawrence and I became immediate friends, but he moved back to New York two weeks after I arrived, one reason being that he was angered by Teddy's racket-making, another being that, although he was gay, he could not stand the "mean young gays" who live on South Beach. I know my other neighbors even less well than I knew Tracey, whom I barely knew. I am a gregarious person, but my neighbors live on their own little planets and want to keep it that way. Indeed, when I greeted a neighbor who lives in the front building, and said that I did not know my neighbors.

"I don't want to know my neighbors," she said and abruptly turned her back on me and walked away. I only know her from her orgasms when her boyfriend visits – she is a screamer.

I no longer greet the two men who live in one of the back studios, as they are exceedingly sullen and gave me the impression that I am a gringo they would rather kill than say hello to. There is one courteous fellow downstairs: Carmichael, a bodybuilder, nightclub doorman, and youth worker, but I rarely see him because he works day and night. And there is my sole neighbor upstairs, whom I rarely see because he works nights as well; thankfully, he is the quietest man on earth, and he put a welcome mat and plants on our shared stairwell instead of the customary bags of garbage.

Now then, since the ubiquitous "I" is our main subject, I am eager to say something about my own appreciation. What do I appreciate about my physical environment? I appreciate the beach most of all. If it were not for the beach itself, South Beach would be nearly worthless, at least in my opinion as a frustrated beach bum. Well, yes, I appreciate the Art Deco architecture when the sun falls upon the pastels in a certain way, although I consider the ornamental style superficial and cheap on the whole. As for function, many of the buildings were Army barracks during the war and should have been torn down long before being put on the historic preservation list. My apartment complex is unusual, not Art Deco ornamented. I appreciate my studio, but I liked it better when it was almost bare. I do not require much stuff to be an enormously successful failure. I am leery of owning luxuries, preferring to view them when they are in someone else's possession or when displayed in museums and picture books. For me beauty really is in the mind of the beholder. I am complex within but a minimalist without. I have furnished my studio with a few things from the alley, and with a TV and microwave from the much smaller, hotel room I had lived in before the hotel was purchased by developers. The vulgar residents of that hotel including me were precipitously evicted to make way for the gentry; holdouts had their doors kicked in by off-duty Miami Beach cops – the hotel sits empty two years later. But I got a TV and microwave out of the exchange.

My most useful possession is the used computer my generous friend Darwin gave me after I wrote his 'Manifesto on Cubosurrealism'. I also have plenty of books to appreciate, titles such as *The Deconstruction of Literature, Fathers and Sons, The Way We Never Were, Ten Philosophical Mistakes, The Pursuit of Loneliness, The Success and Failure of Picasso, The Myth of Male Power, Becoming Mona Lisa, The Lonely Crowd, The Man Who Knew Too Much, Great Cons and Con Artists, Magister Ludi,* and *The Skin of Chagrin.*

Tracey was all alone when she suffered her breakdown, too depressed even to reach out to her high priestess, Oprah, perhaps the only person in the world who might have saved her with a talk. Chatting on her cell phone failed to relieve her loneliness, so Tracey had turned it off for good.

Oh, she was so lonely! I remember that *The Pursuit of Loneliness,* copyrighted in 1970, claimed that American culture, with its economy based on greedy individualism, was at the breaking point. The problem with the striving for money is that its value is inflated, from a tool facilitating exchange to a digital symbol of power; thus the lust for easy money distracts people from actually producing and distributing the basic goods and services and the better environment that everyone needs. As for the liberated American woman, she is still manipulated to live for the convenience of men, who still cultivate violence at home and abroad.

Moreover, *The Lonely Crowd*, copyrighted in 1961, suggests that our "other-directed" contemporary individualism may be more flexible but is as conducive to conformity as the "inner-directed" or tradition-bound individualism we associate with the legendary "rugged individual," whose common morality was implanted in early life by authority figures. Now that relative affluence has been obtained for the majority of Americans, the problem is less and less with squeezing out a living from the natural environment, and more and more with profiting from other people, with whom everyone is increasingly in touch by mass media, which of course serves the rigid organizations needed to harness the new flexibility. Rapidly changing fashions instead of enduring morality is the contemporary rule for other-directed people, who are, on the whole, and especially if they are rootless Americans, more friendly, shallow, wasteful and insecure than the inner-directed traditionalist of old. A survey of people on the street and any popular magazine rack, and an audit of casual conversations, belies the notion that contemporary persons are unique individuals in any way – if anything, they have been over-socialized. We are virtually zombies, possessed consumers. We have more and more things to choose from, but the choices are not ours; we want something else besides all that, but we really don't know what that is, or quite how to get it, and we lose faith.

One of Tracey's letters to herself, penned shortly before her departure, is instructive: "I want to be proud. What is pride? What is being proud? What do I want my definition of pride to be? Pride is in visible, external success, the proof of greatness. Since I want pride, I lack pride and must really hate myself. I want greatness but am not great. If most of the people in the world died today or went to prison unfulfilled, I believe they might still be great, but they were unable to recognize their greatness. Is that the meaning of failure? For me it is because I know these processes, I know the secrets of the universe and I still screw up. I don't care about those people who don't know they are great – I care about me. What is it all for? We could die in a week and what is it all for? What do I want it to be for? I wanted to be able to be happy in every moment, to choose stuff in every moment and have that lead to greatness. Why, why, why? For the fun of it, that's why. I wanted to feel that way, to have joy, and I saw famous people feeling that way, having fun. Everybody wants money and fame so I figured that if I could have that it would lead to joy. So I wanted to be great. If there is no proof of greatness then what is the point of being here? Why bother? Because they tell me all this stupid crap, like I can create anything I want and am a genius creator, et cetera et cetera. And then I look at my stupid life and the fact that I can't even exist without some weird, intense pattern of thought taking over, and I sometimes think we are all so full of crap, so full of crap that life is really futile."

I have retrieved a few of Tracey's things and have suitably positioned them around my place to get to know her better. In addition to her secret stash, I have her big brown teddy bear named Penelope, a Voodoo charm, the dry-eraser board, a cute little bowl, a large mug decorated all around with the image of a one-million-dollar bill, fifteen boxes of tea, and books entitled *The Millionaire Mind, Pathfinder, Self Matters, What Color is Your Parachute, What Color is Your Parachute and Basic Spanish Grammar*, along with representative samples of her subscriptions to O – The Oprah Magazine and Oxygen.. The Salvation Army will pick up the rest of Tracey's stuff next Friday. The stuffed chair is a prize but the neighbors do not want it, as it is very large for small studios and rooms, and one would need two men and a truck to get to move it.

Tracey's somewhat dated books are in mint condition, as if they have never been cracked. Opening *The Millionaire Mind* at random, we find this tidbit from a multimillionaire's mouth, for digestion by success-seekers: "We feel power and control.... It's a sense of power. You become king within reason. I have a small corporation.... Those that don't agree with me can resign...very democratic."

The Pathfinder's subtitle is, 'How to Choose or Change Your Career for a Lifetime of Satisfaction and Success.' We learn that "part of the reason so few people have truly satisfying lives is that they simply do not have tools adequate to the task of designing such a life." The author provides us with the tools, after noting that "most of us would not be willing to live such a life for very long, even if we could design it."

Self Matters addressed the subject of 'Creating Your Life from the Inside Out.' The author assigns us our first task on page 63: "Beginning right now, with only the second chapter of this book, I am asking you to take a huge 'time out' from this scramble you call life, and to focus on the one doing the scrambling: you. I am asking you, demanding of you that you focus fully and unapologetically on you."

What Color is Your Parachute would have us know that there is a job out there for you: 'Write This on Your Forehead, There Are Always Vacancies Out There,' reads the rubric on page 19 of the 2006 edition. As for Basic Spanish Grammar, often essential for getting a low-paying job in Miami – 'bilingual (Spanish) required' reads the want ad –

practice makes perfect. If Tracey did not read these pristine condition books, those of us who did read them and are still stuck in a rut may not blame her: we known what to do but don't do it, for that is the very nature of the rut.

Honore de Balzac would certainly appreciate Tracey's million-dollar coffee mug in the wee hours. I'm drinking my coffee from it as I write, and with this wish, that Tracey Flagler return from the beyond to sue me for stealing her secret. I shall raise the defense that her last testament left her estate to finders-keepers. And then I shall gladly cut her a settlement check for the cool million dollars she wanted so badly that she did not notice it beneath her feet, just as I did not look down at the roll of hundred-dollar bills my right foot stepped on the other day while strolling along Washington Avenue – I cursed at the felt impediment and kept on walking; a homeless man ran across the street to pick it up the money: "Oh, my God!" he exclaimed. God, indeed!

I was taught not to look down, but to keep my head always held high, and to look upwards, at empty space, when I prayed – perhaps that is why I have faith in Nothing instead of in things. I appreciate the fact that that poor man who looked downwards got the bankroll – I did look downwards at Equinox South Beach one day during my free trial and found a $100 bill on the gym's floor. I appreciate even more the fact that my studio has six windows. I appreciate the marvelous webs spun between the palms and the buildings by the crab spiders. I appreciate the two little trees the landlord planted outside my window. They were knocked down by hurricanes several times, but they took root during the last two, untroubled seasons. Butterflies, duly camouflaged with yellow wings, flit about the yellow flowering leaves on a background of dark green leaves, and a noisy blue jay has taken up residence in one tree – when I answer with a song from my flute, he takes off for a while. I used to look out of my window above the bathtub when showering, to appreciate the sight of Tracey's favored fluffy kitties sitting in her window – stray cats also sunned themselves on her doorstep, dreaming of another bite to eat from her generous hand.

Yes, I appreciate South Beach, my apartment, and the things in it. I imagine Tracey Flagler felt some joy in her circumstances, just as I have joyful moments in mine. But who is Tracey Flagler, and who am I? That remains to be seen.

Tracey's Fun

Although I barely knew Tracey Flagler, I miss her now that she is gone. I used to give her a goofy smile when we passed in the yard or on the street. I tried to converse with her, but she had little or no time to spare, perhaps because my conversation tends to run into long, off-the-cuff essays, and she had other things to do than to listen to a monologue. No doubt she had heard every line a man could throw out, anyway. She was, I found out, the outstanding beauty who stood in for Charlize Theron in the romantic movie, *Sweet November*, about a woman who lures a different man every month into her arms to help him out, avoiding long-term commitments all the while because she is terminally ill. Charlize, we might remember, was once rated the "Sexiest Woman Alive" by Esquire.

It is with that in mind that I clipped Charlize's photograph from the magazine's cover and pinned it up on my wall. When I gaze at the image of the sexiest woman alive, I imagine that she is really Tracey, my own nice girl next door, so to speak. After all, if it were not for the slings and arrows of fortune and other quirks of fate, Tracey would be a movie star today, and I could very well say to whoever would listen, "I knew Tracey Flagler well. She was my neighbor," whenever she appeared on the Oprah Winfrey Show. She would tell Oprah that she, Tracey Flagler, was just lucky, and Oprah would disagree with her, just as she disagreed with Charlize Theron in their talk published in Oprah Magazine back in November 2005:

"You keep saying you're lucky," Oprah told Charlize, "and I can't take it. You're not lucky. You are blessed and graced. Even the word blessed doesn't capture the bigness of it. When you are in alignment with the divine current of your life, that's when that thing people call luck happens."

My dear Tracey would reply, "Oprah, you really flatter me, to think that God has personally graced and blessed me because I became aligned with the Divine Current, just as you did before you got your two and a half billion dollars, while those who fail don't become aligned with it, even though they believe in it, watch your show, read Abraham-Hicks and Seth and Conversations with God, and pray ever so desperately to the source of the divine current! Thank you! It's so much better to bathe in the divine current and be graced and blessed by divine being than to be graced and blessed by Lady Luck."

Ah, if only I had slept with the sexiest woman in the world before she became rich and famous, if only I had taken a dozen tawdry photos of the carnal process, I might have exposed all and gotten myself blessed and graced with a hundred grand.

'O, my, my dear O, thanks to you, my imagination is running away with me! On second thought, I think I am not that sort of person. Alas, if only I could align myself with the Divine Currency of the Central Banker and go with the Cash Flow, I would be swimming in charitable units of exchange. 'O, Dear O, please send me two million dollars over the next year and I shall split it with Tracey, give half of my cut to St. Jude's Children's Hospital so more kids can be cured of cancer, and shall support my literary gift with the other half.

We should treat people a lot better when they are here instead of making legends of them after they are gone, but since I missed the opportunity, I have the legend. I can see from Tracey's frantic scrawling in the diaries I recovered from her studio that we had a few things in common, things we might have shared in this limbo called South Beach. Indeed, we might even have been famous friends. It occurs to me that kindred spirits tend to commune in the same places although they might not be formally aware of their communality. It is as if we were attracted to a place by underlying geomagnetic forces. South Beach might one day become a subtropical Findhorn for New Age weirdos

Tracey Flagler loved South Beach, but its many alienated residents lack the sunny disposition of their sunny environment, and, on the whole, they prefer to keep their distance with a frown. Only ingratiating beggars dare smile. Everybody go ahead and smile, then. After all, everybody got naked at the Sagamore Art Hotel for Spencer Tunick's installation on October 8, 2007, so why not get together for one big smile? Do we not all want something for nothing? Don't we want unconditional love? Some say the father-god had stuff to begin with, but we sons of god prefer to believe that the world was created out of nothing and handed to us on a silver platter. Furthermore, we would supplant our father and treat ourselves as gods in our own right. After all, we are waited on hand and foot as babies, so handouts are naturally expected. Infants are eventually given good reason to fear that more stuff shall not be forthcoming if they are too demanding, but a smile in lieu of outraged cries will often do the trick, or at least belay a smack on the bottom.

Perhaps I myself am at bottom a bum, for I unwittingly smile broadly from time to time, seemingly for no reason at all, as if I were a baby if not the village idiot. I should know better, but I cannot help smiling and kidding around. If looks could kill, I would be dead: I smiled at the world while sitting on the patio of Starbucks just last Sunday. A man got up, walked over to me, said nothing, and stared into my eyes with unutterable hatred. I don't know, maybe he mistook me for a war criminal who had caused his family and friends to be tortured and murdered; but I figured he was a murderer on vacation, perhaps looking for a celebrity to kill, so I walked away with my smile even though I felt a self-defensive urge to hit him over the head with a heavy patio chair several times until he went on a permanent vacation. But he had confronted the wrong man this time, the Nobody who apparently looks like somebody, a man who had better things to do than to engage in a so-called Darwinian struggle for the survival of the fittest at Starbucks.

South Beach Hispanics and Jews seem more secure and somewhat happier than the alienated lots. Hispanics prize their families and are more familiar with their familiars than the run-of-the-mill atomized individual. Since Spain was first to seize Florida from its aborigines, Hispanics feel they have a right to South Florida at the very least. Many Hispanics work for a pittance on South Beach and live on the mainland, but a few poor Latinos cling to South Beach for what it's worth; and a number of rich Latinos like South Beach well enough to maintain fabulous quarters here and there. Jews cleave to their families and familiars as well. By the way, investors, Jews still own a goodly portion of South Beach, mostly for sale at bargain prices, in case you are interested. But the large Jewish population has fled, making way for gentile gentrification.

The gentiles, contrary to their namesake, are not clannish. We might call them pagans or villains or heathen, but they are not country comrades or tight-knit villagers and they do not adhere to sacred hearths. They are, in truth, neo-barbarian individualists. Gringos and goyim bring the suspiciousness of their parochial towns and the angry isolation of their respective cities to South Beach with them. They seek refuge from the barbarous, unwholesome war of all against all most prevalent on the East Coast, where Mars rules, or rather Thor-Zeus. They want relief from the insanity or unwholesomeness they cannot help but to bring with them as unwanted baggage – no matter where you go, there you are. Mind you that South Beach is famous for the craziness of its residents, call it eccentricity if you wish to be politically correct, particularly among those abject vagrants who flock to South Beach to live publicly and panhandle under the protective wing of its permissive authorities – a city commissioner who opposed an anti-panhandling ordinance referred to the crazed characters as a favorite tourist attraction.

People flock to South Beach to relax and have fun, to take a break from the rat race and puritan work ethic and inhibiting moral codes, to do what they want to do to please their own selves one way or another. Bacchanalia it is not, but perversion is appreciated and tolerated. We all want to have fun. Many of us will never grow up. Our gurus preach infantilism or childishness, a return to the inner child, the kid within; we are to return to our origin, the aboriginal fountain of youth within, and live in the eternal moment, free of guilt about the past and anxiety for the future. Let us return to our true nature; let us be innocent babies: the negative old farts always die off, and the positive-attitude babies always win. Yes, indeed, we would like to return to the security of the source, to the womb, where nothing has to be done, where we can relax. At the same time we associate fun with absolute freedom from restrictions, with the feeling of power we had as omnipotent infants once relieved of the birth trauma. We believe life should be an eternal vacation, that the whole point and final cause of living is, in fine, to have fun.

Oh, joy, joy, and more joy! If only the point of life as advertised could be had, if only the instant Now were not spurious, there would be no end to the fun! The advertisements for tourist meccas like South Beach reinforce high expectations for relaxing and having fun. Even Islamists find South Florida irresistible: they cover up the breast of Madonna suckling baby Jesus in the picture in their motel room with a towel, and gravitate to strip clubs where their appetite for metaphysical virgins is whetted. Alas, the service class must work hard for fun, and they do not always work for the fun of it.

"All I want is fun and excitement," Tracey Flagler scrawled in her diary after a hard night's work as a food server. "I want to sense that my life is amazing. It is all for fun, that's what the purpose life is, to have fun. I can have anything imaginable. I can create anything I want. I am in this body because I chose it, and I can leave it any time I want and have another body if I so choose, for I am really everlasting life. All I have to do is to relax and accept joy, joy, and more joy, the joy that is mine because the universe adores me for being one of its bright stars. If I can't have fun doing something, then I shouldn't do it. This planet will be gone tomorrow so I shall have fun on it today. I will just relax and enjoy my vacation here, and then I shall vacation on another planet. May this happy vacation last forever, and it will do so because I wish it would. Wow, what a great idea, of being on vacation eternally, of taking a permanent vacation from all the troubles stupid people occupy themselves with. Life then would be so much more fun and exciting and amazing! Inner Being, please steer me to what is easy and fun and helps me to connect to you where I enjoy the forces that make life fun. Please steer me to fun friends, and to fun relationships that are easy and long and passionate and fun."

Tracey thought she might be befriended by rich and famous celebrities at the fabulous party hotels where she worked. Perhaps her foot would fit the proverbial glass slipper. After that, she supposed, life would be a ball. By virtue of her association with celebrities, she would enjoy celebrity status herself, and then others would hang on her every word. Celebrities had the power she craved, and they obviously could relax and have a great deal of fun. Powerful people as well as dominant apes must at least appear to be relaxed in order to maintain their superior status before an adulating or cringing audience. And of course democracies are supposed to be more fun for everyone concerned.

Many celebrities are talented indeed, and they have worked hard for what they have, but most notably the notables or Names have won the great popularity contest. The Name is the claim to fame, and fame is sufficient authority in itself. Essentially, celebrities are members of the power elite who are celebrated simply because of the positions they occupy. As a matter of fact, they may be far from wise and may even be flagrant fools or perverse clowns if not drunks, dope addicts, and wife beaters. Whatever prestige they might have on a small scale is inflated by the national spotlight. Prestige is a dominating power; it paralyzes the critical faculty and fills the adulator of idols with astonishment and respect if not awe. Wealth is not the only form of power – a penniless saint may influence the world – but the prestige of celebrities more often than not is boosted by the perception of wealth, by the power to obtain whatever money can buy; and that includes, first and foremost, fun.

Status is a psychological place where the power elite meet. Conventiclers do not conspire in that virtual space, but there is an abiding interest in maintaining power over the populace. Conservative snobs and mobsters have their private clubs and secluded resorts; they do not want publicity, for it might call into question their prestige. "The moment prestige is called into question it ceases to be prestige," observed Gustave LeBon in his groundbreaking study of crowds. "The gods and men who have kept their prestige for long have never tolerated discussion. For the crowd to admire it, it must have been kept at a distance." But celebrities must be seen to be celebrated in this great democratic republic of ours. South Beach seemed to be a great backdrop for the public display of the sweet life beautiful celebrities are supposed to live every day. But then a man celebrated for making celebrities look good was slain on the doorstep of his posh Ocean Drive mansion by a madman. It dawned on celebrities that some of the crazy people who flock to South Beach to enjoy the permissive atmosphere are exceedingly dangerous to the welfare of the elite. So celebrities withdrew from South Beach. The ones who do appear on occasion usually keep their distance – a famous hip-hopping athlete might get drunk, pull out his pecker and urinate on Washington Avenue.

The fear of celebrity-killers greatly reduced the chance of persons like me and Tracey Flagler of meeting celebrities on South Beach and being recognized by them as the great people we really are, people whom it would be fun for them to know and to adopt into their fun-loving circles. If we knew them better, we might have discovered that we were already having more fun than they did, but just didn't know it. But that wouldn't have kept us from having more fun than a barrel of monkeys with them. Mind you that a monkey's grin does not necessarily mean he's frightened and angry.

Tracey's Chagrin

"Right now I am really mad," Tracey Flagler, my proverbially Nice Girl Next Door, had scribbled furiously in her diary. "I want a million dollars right away. I want to be independently wealthy so that I do not have to do anything. My life just seems to be so stupid sometimes that I no longer want eternity. Who wants eternal stupidity? Eternity sounds so exhausting! I want amazing things to happen. I want to see myself as amazing. I am angry that I have to work tonight. I am mad that I have to support myself. I just don't want to do anything anymore. I wish I were DEAD. I want to be free right now, and I mean right NOW, or DEAD."

Give me liberty or give me death – perhaps the two are one and the same, so let me have the cash. Tracey finally freed herself from going to work. I noticed that she had not fed the dozen or so alley cats that showed up at her door regularly. I glanced discreetly into her window from my bathroom window next door, saw her nude form on the bed, and surmised that she was sleeping. The next day I looked again; her body was in exactly the same position, and likewise the day after. Something was wrong with that picture. I went across the way, up the flight of stairs to her apartment, knocked on her door and looked into her window. Her body did not move. I tried the door; it was open; her prized cats, the fluffy ones she kept inside, did not race around as usual, but put their heads down and growled sorrowfully.

The odor was ghastly. It was a good thing she had put out plenty of food for her cats, I thought, or they would have eaten her according to the rule, Food eats food. A note to our landlord was pinned on the wall, asking him to get rid of whatever he found in the apartment. After official inquiries were completed and the apartment unsealed, he told Tracey's fellow tenants to take whatever they wanted before the Salvation Army truck arrived. I was the last to take my pick, but I found a fortune that had been neglected and tossed into garbage bags, namely her literary remains, along with several charming items that have occult properties, and other things I have described elsewhere. I found a book outline that she had penned on 35 pages of an Eden Roc Hotel note pad. The book would include a chapter on reincarnation, but she had written "DELETE" beside 'Ch.7 – Reincarnation'. Who knows where Tracey is now, or whether she exists at all?

The answer to that question was imagined in my dream last night. I saw her reflection in a bubble that popped up on an ocean of milk. She had resurfaced in a motel room – San Diego Motor Inn, read the neon sign flashing just outside the window, casting an eerie red light across the room. Her lithe, alabaster form was stark naked except for a big black cat she held across her chest as she stood by the bed. Music from Madonna's latest album was playing on the clock radio. An elegant leather briefcase was on the stand at the foot of the bed. She put the cat down, exposing her enchanting bosom, bent over and opened the briefcase. It was full of money – exactly one million dollars, I instantly calculated in my dream. I was both aroused and amazed by the spectacle. She looked up at me and smiled. Somehow I knew that I could have anything I wanted if I would squeeze her marvelous breasts at the same time, one in each hand, and make a wish. She glided towards me, hips swaying with the music, fulsome lips slightly parted. Now if someone comes at you with their lips slightly parted, you have to kiss them, so I intended to do just that, and to fondle her breasts as well, and of course to enjoy the joy within her at the same time, but as she came near and I eagerly looked at her flat tummy, I awoke with a start – she had no navel! What did it mean?

Unless our lives are dreams we have wished upon ourselves, dreams rarely come true. If only I had kissed her lips and squeezed her magic breasts and wished that I would never wake up to this reality, I might have forgotten the difference between dreams and reality, and enjoyed an orgasmic life with the woman of my dreams – the existential ace cannot exist alone: there must always be another for number one to be. But one must be careful what one wishes for, and it might be best not to wish for anything at all lest the source completely dries up. Tracey's breasts might have shrunk with my every wish, just as did the skin of the wild ass in Balzac's instructive story, 'Le Peau de Chagrin – The Skin of Chagrin.'

. Raphael of Valentine, the impoverished young protagonist of Balzac's story, had discovered the secret of success in the human will, and he had in fact drafted a seminal work on the subject. In sum, he believed in the power of passionate thinking to achieve anything one wants. But his grinding poverty belied his theory, or rather some obscure fault in him rendered him unable to prove it true in his case, so one day he resolved to drown himself in the river Seine, after losing his last gold piece at the gambling parlor. As disaffected youth knows very well, suicide is the most obvious solution to life's problems, but most of us survive the troubling years.

"There is something great and terrible about suicide," observed Balzac in Chagrin. "Most people's downfalls are not dangerous; they are like children who have not far to fall, and cannot injure themselves; but when a great nature is dashed down, he is bound to fall from a height. He must have been raised almost to the skies; he has caught glimpses of some heaven beyond his rich. Vehement must be the storms by which compel a soul to seek for peace from the trigger of a pistol."

The late Tracey Flagler, who was an aspiring author among other things, certainly would have appreciated Raphael's predicament as much as I do: "How much young power starves and pines away in a garret for want of a friend, for lack of a woman's consolation, in the midst of millions of fellow-creatures, in the presence of a listless crowd that is burdened by its wealth! When one remembers all this, suicide looms large. Between a self-sought death and the abundant hopes which call a man to Paris, God only knows what may intervene; what contending ideas have striven within the soul; what poems have been set aside; what moans and what despair have been repressed; what abortive masterpieces and vain endeavors! Every suicide is an awful poem of sorrow. Where will you find a work of genius floating above the seas of literature that one can compare with this paragraph: Yesterday, at four o'clock, a young woman threw herself into the Seine from the Pont des Arts."

As Raphael treads his melancholic path to the river, he encounters two beggars along the way, on old man and a child; they pled for his charity, he flings his remaining small change at them, and continues towards his fate. But he decides to wait until dark to forever extinguish his passionate will, lest he be seen and fished out of the water alive by the suicide-prevention institution, 'THE ROYAL HUMANE SOCIETY'S APPARATUS', which has a shed nearby. Much to his posthumous dishonor, the record of his attempt would then be published in the paper.

Wherefore Raphael entered an antique store to pass the time, and there he eventually encounters the proprietor, a centenarian, one of those types that serve artists so well as models for Moses:

"The craftiness of an inquisitor, revealed in those curving wrinkles and creases that wound about his temples, indicated a profound knowledge of life. There was no deceiving this man, who seemed to possess a power of detecting the secrets of the wariest hearth. The wisdom and the moral codes of every people seemed gathered up in his passive face, just as all the productions of the globe had been heaped up in his dusty showrooms. He seemed to possess a power of detecting the secrets of the wariest heart."

The wise old Jew was iconoclast who wanted nothing, therefore he wound up with it all, including an antique shop full of curious from his carefree travels all over the world. We venture to invent a maxim here – if it has already been penned by another, our plagiary is pardonable: He who wants for nothing has everything.

"I have attained everything," uttered the old man, "because I have known how to despise all things. My one ambition has been to see. Is not Sight in a manner Insight? And to have knowledge or insight, is not that to have instinctive possession? To be able to discover the very substances of fact and to unite its essence to our essence? Of material possession what abides with you but an idea? Think, then, how glorious must be the life of a man who can stamp all realities upon his thought, place the springs of happiness within himself, and draw thence uncounted pleasures in idea, unsoiled by earthly stains. Thought is the key to all treasures; the miser's gains are ours without his cares.... The true millions lie here," he said, striking his forehead.

The wizened wise merchant had something in store, a curio that he felt would be most suitable for Raphael's distraught state: "Without compelling you to entreat me, without making you blush for it...I will make you richer, more powerful, and of more consequence than a constitutional king.... Turn round, look at that leather skin," he went on, using his lamp to illuminate the talisman, a portion skin from a wild ass, stamped with the Seal of Solomon, no bigger than a fox's skin, gleaming on the opposite wall, upon which something was inscribed in Sanskrit. Raphael, highly educated as he was, translated the exotic script into English:

Possessing Me Thou Shalt Possess All Things, But Thy Life Is Mine, For God Has So Willed It. Wish, And Thy Wishes Shall Be Fulfilled; But Measure Thy Desires, According To The Life That Is In Thee. This Is Thy

Life, With Each Wish I Must Shrink Even As Thy Own Days. Wilt Thy Have Me? Take Me. God Will Harken Unto Thee. So Be It!

Raphael asked the merchant if it was some sort of joke, or, then again, was it an enigma. The old coot responded, in part, "Before you came here, you made up your mind to kill yourself, but all at once a mystery fills your mind, and you think no more about death. You child!" And, "I am a centenarian with a couple of years to spare, and a millionaire to boot. Misery was the making of me, ignorance had made me learned. I will tell you in a few words the great secret of human life. By two instinctive processes man exhausts the springs of life within him. Two verbs cover all the forms which these two causes of death may take – To Will and To have your Will.... To Will consumes us, and To have our Will destroys us, but To Know steeps our feeble organisms in perpetual calm. In me Thought has destroyed Will, so that Power is relegated to the ordinary functions of my economy. In a word, it is not in the heart which can be broken, nor in the senses that become deadened, but it is in the brain that cannot waste away and survives everything else, that I have set my life." Moreover, "Is not the utmost brightness of the ideal world soothing to us, while the lightest shadows of the physical world annoy? Is not knowledge the secret of wisdom? And what is folly but a riotous expenditure of Will or Power?"

"Very good then, a life of riotous expense for me!" Raphael rebelliously exclaimed. I had resolved my existence into thought and study, and yet they have not even supported me. I am not gulled by a speech worthy of Swedenborg, nor by your Oriental amulet...." Raphael then proceeded to wish upon the Skin of Chagrin for, in short, a life of boon companions for the riotous enjoyment of fine wine, passionate women, and, it goes without saying, song, culminating in no less than orgasmic joy: "I bid this enigmatic power to concentrate all delights for me in one single joy. Yes, I must comprehend every pleasure of earth and heaven in the final embrace that is to kill me."

"Joy, joy, joy, joy, joy...!" Tracey Flagler had reiterated longingly during the lonely lucubration before her disappointing demise. The wishes Raphael made came true, and each truth shrank the magic skin along with his life, for that skin of a wild ass was his own ass, so to speak. But Tracey's wishes did not come true. Her heart shriveled in despair, and she overdosed herself with the drugs her psychiatrist had prescribed to relieve her melancholy, having saved up several prescriptions for a dire emergency. If only she had met Raphael, and he had become her Balzac, they might have lived a longer life on the average, and had a great deal of fun in the meantime. No doubt the bejeweled Madame Tracey of Valentine would have hosted a most charming Parisian salon. She would not have the billions of an Oprah, but powerful gentlemen would marvel at her breathtaking beauty, as if she were Madame Recamier herself, and, like Madame Recamier's great friend Madame de Staël, Madame Tracey would probably enchant the likes of Napoleon with her popular gift of gab. Madame de Staël's books are rarely read today, and are roundly criticized as mediocre, but none other summed up the society of her time so well. Madame de Staël and Napoleon were unwilling to share power over the minds of influential men, so he exiled her – Madame Recamier was charged with the crime of visiting her. Her exile gave her cause to contemplate suicide in her tome, 'Reflections on Suicide.'

"Inordinate misery makes people think about suicide," wrote Baronne Anne Louise Germaine de Staël-Holsten (nëe Necker). "We need not be afraid of devoting too much time to this subject –it is at the heart of mankind's whole moral organization. I flatter myself that I can offer a few new insights into the motives that lead us to suicide, and those that should turn us away from it."

Like everyone else, I have considered suicide, the only absolute freedom one has. First of all, I desperately opined, it is impossible for god to kill himself. But what could god do with eternity but to create something to break the boredom? I was moved to become the greatest author the world would ever or never know, the author who managed to cremate himself with his own works. At present I am writing the second draft of the seventh volume of my planned fifty-volume suicide note. To whom am I writing? Unhappy people.

"Unhappy people are the ones to write for," wrote Madame de Staël. "People who have the good things of the world learn only from their experience, and consider abstract ideas on any topic nothing but wasted time. Sufferers are different: reflection is their safest refuge. Isolated from the distractions of society by misfortune, they examine themselves like an invalid tossing on his bed of pain, seeking the least agonizing position they can find."

"It would be so nice if I had enough reasons to want to be here," reads an entry in Tracey's diary. "The idea that there are an infinite number of reasons to live thrilled me at first, but I don't have one of them for myself. Right now I HATE, HATE, HATE – I HATE being alive – I want to be alive but it sucks to be alive –I HATE this culture based on the fun I don't have – I HATE drugs and alcohol – I HATE Abraham – I HATE myself for not taking responsibility for him – I HATE being sad all the time – I wish I were dead and I wish Abraham were dead so I could stop loving him – I HATE thinking that I will not love someone so much again – I'm trying to tap into true love and the humans like Oprah Winfrey and Madonna and Jerry and Esther Hicks and Neale Donald Walsch and Jane Roberts and Robert Butts and Pat Rodegast and Judith Stanton and Napoleon Hill, people who have found true love – I know in my heart I'm so good but I HATE myself for not having their fun. Have I had fun here? That is the question. No, I am not having fun now. That is what all the reasons to live are really for, to have FUN! Do I want to be here? No, I wish I were dead, dead, DEAD! But my book makes me feel better. I have fun when writing it. I would have fun teaching people JOY. I know Oprah would love my book, and she would have me on her show, and I would have plenty of money and be secure, and I could finally relax, take a permanent vacation from all these stupid people who don't have any imagination, who don't know they can create their own planets and live on them with their own lovers, like my Abraham, and then I would have fun all the time. Joy, joy, joy, JOY would be forever mine! "

If only Tracey could be around to see Honoré de Balzac appear on the Oprah Winfrey show: Oh what wisdom he would impart to our bourgeois world! It is a world that was already well on its way in Balzac's day. Balzac cut his literary teeth anonymously, as a potboiler formula writer. The formulas are rather simple, rooted in the motivational principles of human nature, but they are better kept a trade secret, for an audience loves to be deceived, and a disillusioned audience will not maintain the trade. Love does not abhor a secret, nor does Oprah, but she would not have to be embarrassed with the revelation that our masterful novelist was a profligate fraud burdened by insurmountable debts due to his spendthrift ways. She would no doubt appreciate a confident man who was able to exchange novels for his staggering debts even before the novels were conceived let alone written.

Nonfiction authors lie a lot to tell a little truth. Great novelists lie a little to tell great truths. In any event, if it were not for the human imagination, next to nothing would get said or done. Honoré de Balzac, like his bureaucratic father before him, fancied himself as entitled to a title, but also the fun life that goes with it. He naturally fell in love with a fabulously wealthy Russian countess, who was so kind as to provide funds from time to time, and to finally marry him after putting her fortune in a trust he could not get at, but who in the end was more interested in shopping for jewelry than in his deteriorating health, as that was his problem, not hers. Oprah Winfrey would probably be much to his liking, and even the more so given their mutual interest in the occult. He wanted millions and lost a great deal of other people's money trying to get them, but money was not the cause of the monomania he attributed to his characters; rather, there was some sort of energy, an essential force or elemental power underlying reality, and, despite his business failures, he thought that thought concentrated by that force was bound to succeed for good or ill. Yes, the occult power of thinking could be misdirected to negative as well as positive ends hence could be an enormously destructive power – monists speak enthusiastically of the creative-destructive power.

Balzac's own life was a grandiose wish for love, fame and fortune. His pursuit of happiness despite every failure unto his premature end, has blessed our self-loving, money-grubbing culture with an everlasting self-portrait of great beauty. At the end of the day, human history seems to be a mistake for which we have due cause for chagrin. On the other hand, since this is the best of all possible worlds because it is the only one immediately available, we have cause for joy as well, for without the great expectations that lead to so many disappointments, life would not be worth living.

Tracey Flagler misunderstood eternity, I opined today as I relished some of the chocolate I retrieved from her apartment. Eternity is exhausting, but only in the sense that it relieves us of time altogether, hence we are relieved therewith of our anxiety over the future. Eternity is not time, it has no moments. Eternity does not go on forever and ever: Eternity is immovable. Eternity is that Better Place funereal preachers refer to in order to console the living. There is no stuff to want or to worry about in that placeless place. There is neither North nor South, nor East nor West, in eternity: The rivers of milk and honey in the East and the emerald trees laden with precious gems in the West are exotic fictions piously designed to lure the vulgar onto the exoteric paths that converge at the occluded center of the universe, the center that is and is not, the center that is at once everywhere and nowhere, the pointless point of it all. May we enjoy everything besides the point.

"Take me, and God will harken unto thee!" If the Skin of Chagrin has been wizened by desire down to nothing, then may we have faith in Nothing, the Negatively Existent One. Only Nothing is perfect. The rest is for naught, so let us have as much fun as we can, even though we might suffer for it. Perhaps if we cared less about fun, and stopped making ourselves miserable for the want of it, we would have a lot more of it.

Tracey's Madonna - A Séance

"I want to be part of the pulse of life, not a weird and ashamed outrider," Tracey had scribbled in her confessional journal some time before she left South Beach for good. "I want to be proud of being here, knowing that I can be connected to the source and deliberately choose and control my focus just like I am doing right now with this pen and paper. I am proud of people with HUGE physical success, like Madonna, and that would make me proud of myself. I want others to be proud of my success as I teach them how to focus and get exactly what they want. I wish so much that I had physical proof of my power to create success. Why? So I could relax. Why would I relax? Because I had succeeded."

If only I had known about my neighbor's dire emotional strait before I had found her dead from an overdose in her apartment, I would have invited her over and channeled George Berkeley for her edification. Then she would have known that one does not have to die to get rid of physical obstructions, for physical objects do not really exist, therefore she could have remained alive and succeeded without such stuff once she was convinced that the goods she wanted were within her. She could have been a successful failure in material terms. Indeed, she could have been all-powerful and instantly successful without a thing to show for it. But alas, the foolish commonsense notion, that matter exists, and that plenty of matter or the money to buy it must be had to prove one's worth in this great nation of ours, persisted in her mind, despite her transcendental inclination towards what she called the source, the source in which she supposed she would completely relax and enjoy in particular the absolute joy she craved so much that she would rather die without it.

Yes, Tracey thought she would have to cop a lot of stuff to make a buy; but deep down within she knew better. She knew that all the stuff in the world would not buy her the fix she really wanted, and in the end she chose the fatal alternative and left her world behind. While rummaging through her apartment after she passed, I found a dog-eared and heavily underlined copy of the transcript of Oprah Winfrey's September 16, 2003 conversation with one of her idols, Madonna, wherein Madonna presented her new, post-cabala side. That the old, material-girl side persisted on the other side of the coin was evident in her apparent belief that stuff really exists:

"MADONNA. Basically, the idea is that I have all of these things that money can buy, but I realized that those aren't the things that make you happy, that make you feel fulfilled, and – and that nothing in the material world will ever make us happy."

The material girl noticed something was missing – her fans may be glad that she realized it after she got rich instead of before. She was not in charge of her life. She was defined by her circumstances; she did not know what her place in it all was. In fine she was a successful shipwreck. And now she is finally getting her island together. The birth of her daughter gave her cause to wonder what she would teach her, and it dawned on her that she did not know what to say for sure. She found the popular version of cabala and she learned that people are personally responsible for everything that happens to them, whether for good or ill. There exists, Madonna informed Oprah, "an all-giving, all-loving force. You can –you could call it God.... When we disconnect from this force, we – that's when we have chaos...that's when we invite pain and suffering into our lives."

Armed with this finding, Madonna decided to write stories that would teach children to identify with their good side and to consider their bad side as an opponent to be defeated. She would fain teach them "about the laws of cause and effect" and thus inspire them to do good deeds, to give them cause to share, with good effect.

Oprah tentatively approved. She thought the new Madonna seemed to be a gentler, kinder sort of person, and blessed her books on the air, augmenting the fact that whatever Madonna does will sell well.

What was the secret of Madonna's physical success? I asked myself. Well, for one thing, she had a strong will, she was persistent, she never stopped dancing, even after she ripped her innards apart and was sewn back together.

I had no idea who Madonna was when I first saw her taking class at Joy of Movement on Broadway and Lafayette: "Don't you know that song, Borderline?" a dancer responded after I asked, "Who's that girl?"

Madonna let it all hang out, and I liked that. The only tool a dancer needs to do her thing is her body. Of course dance sells sex. What's wrong with that? Aren't we all sex buds? Isn't sex the reason for our existence? That must be why sex feels so good. Shall we not unite one day in a gigantic eternal orgasm? Many of our parents said sex was bad, that we should not do it, that we should not touch our thingies. Naturally boys wanted to be bad and girls wanted to be naughty.

Madonna was your average girl, of average height and build, nothing really spectacular, and she had an average voice, but she put on a damn good show with what she had. She gave you the impression that the average girl could make it if she had the gumption. "This may be crap but our job as dancers is to make it smell good," dance master Luigi liked to say. And Madonna made it smell great. I sympathized with her when the cheap shots found in the dumpster were used to deny her uppity housing at the Dakota: How absurd! Who would want to live where Rosemary's baby was born, anyway? And what hypocrisy! Major dope dealers shared an apartment there.

There are dumb dancers but not all dancers are dumb. Some dancers become doctors of medicine and philosophy and the like, but bookish professional dancers are few and far between. Still, a good dancer has sufficient animal intelligence to survive and move ahead of the pack, and Madonna obviously had plenty of that. But now she wants the permanent wisdom that has somehow been occluded by the dynamic material world. She gave birth to a daughter and named her Binah, and she wants to do the right thing now, to do her duty for the sake of her child. She noticed something was missing. What could that missing something be?

Perhaps she lost her ethical self while winning the world, I speculated. I closed my right eye, rolled my left eyeball upwards towards my third eye, took a deep breath, and whispered as I exhaled: "Spirits, what was Madonna missing?" I felt my left brain going into a light trance as my alter ego became the medium for a spiritual conference: the spirits of Immanuel and Baruch showed up:

IMMANUEL: She was missing her Dear Self. Out of my own love for humanity, a love which is by definition ethical, I am willing to admit that Madonna's care for her child is for the sake of her child and performed out of love for her child and a natural sense of maternal duty. But her love for another self, like anyone's love for other selves besides their own, is essentially selfish. Anyone who loves another should know that she in effect loves herself.

BARUCH: Only the intellectual love of GodNature will liberate her from her bondage to limited selves. Once she understands her circumstances and accepts the necessity of her predicaments, her comprehension of GodNature will be assured and the cabala lore rendered moot. This is, after all, the only world possible, and as such it is the best of all possible worlds.

IMMANUEL: My friend, you are a godless Gottfried.

BARUCH: I beg your pardon?

IMMANUEL: All right, then, which is better: to be raped a hundred times by African pirates, to have one buttock cut off, to run the gauntlet in the Bulgar army, to be excommunicated for monstrous deeds and abominable heresies, to be whipped and hanged in an auto-de-fé, to be dissected, to be slowly smothered by glass dust, to be Sisyphus in Hades heaving his stone forever, to be a galley slave to eternity, or to sit around on your thumbs doing nothing and be bored to death?

BARUCH: Whatever happens to us, it is best to be reasonable and to accept it stoically instead of chasing after rainbows in hopes of finding pots of gold at every end. Our happiness and well-being are not in enslavement to the passions, nor in the pursuit of transitory goods that we believe will make us happy, or in related superstitions, but rather in the harmonious intellectual calisthenics of a perfectly consistent, systematic philosophy.

IMMANUEL: Nothing is perfect.

BARUCH: Only if nothing exists is it perfect. God is confessedly perfect, and therefore Nature must be perfect as well: careful reasoning informs us that Nature and God cannot be conceived as distinct things because then each would be limited by the other; God would have then contradicted himself with Nature, hence God would be imperfect. Wherefore God and Nature are one, as GodNature, and the infinite attributes we perceive are merely the innumerable modes of the perfect Nature of Supreme Being. In fine, the best we can do in the best of all possible worlds is to cultivate our intellectual garden.

IMMANUEL: Cultivating an orchard would be more fruitful, practically speaking. We have natural restraints beyond which our understanding, trained by nature, may not obtain. Metaphysics is impossible because the unknown is inconceivable. The ideal world is an illusion, and to dwell on it, no matter how logically, contradicts reality. The perceived world must exist in its own right; otherwise, we would be unsure of our own existence. Madonna would do well to cultivate her daughter and leave the metaphysical nonsense to the cabalists, or to historians who teach the history of the absurd.

BARUCH: The absurd may lead to her blessed enlightenment. One eventually learns that waiting for Godot or praying to God is to no avail. GodNature is surd or deaf to our pleas, for the world on the whole is already perfect, and when we realize the joke is on us, and laugh out loud, we are freed. I too believe Madonna should attend to her daughter Binah, but in both senses of the name.

IMMANUEL: What does binah mean, again? I know we have spoken on this subject before, about the ten sefirot, and about the belief of certain cabalists that it is our duty to recreate God.

BARUCH: Binah means between, the power to distinguish between ideas. Binah is the third of ten sefirot, the womb of understanding, associated of course with the power of understanding.

IMMANUEL: Aha, the analytic. And then Madonna may help others pick up the sparkling shards and put Humpty Dumpty back together again so the cannon may be set upon the wall to defend us from self-contradiction. Once this task has been completed by all, paradise shall be fully restored. However that may be, it is better to presume that God exists transcendentally and to do the 613 mitzvahs rather than sit on our thumbs and exercise our imaginations.

BARUCH: We do nothing on our own. Madonna along with the rest of us shall proceed as determined.

IMMANUEL: She shall do what is willed, whether that will be her own or not. At least I give individual liberty the benefit of the doubt, my friend. Unfortunately for the humanity I love so well, everyone does what they will and no one really obeys the stern command of duty to do the right thing no matter what. The thing that Madonna feels is missing is her Dear Self, and the reason she misses it is because she, like everyone else, is basically selfish, but she has been preoccupied with performing for other people, the fans she loves, and that has distracted her from the real object of her love, her Dear Self. We shall find that her love for her fans is for her own sake, if we analyze it carefully enough and synthesize the results. Unfortunately, there is no such thing as virtue anywhere in the world, for every performance is motivated by what one wants for her Dear Self, whether she knows it or not. When actions are performed for one's own reasons or causes, it makes no difference whether they are benevolently directed towards other selves or greedily directed towards one's dearest self: in either case the actions are not, by definition, ethical, hence are not virtuous.

BARUCH: Immanuel, you are too cynical!

IMMANUEL: No, I'm realistic, a cool observer of the truth of the matter at hand.

BARUCH: So cool that your colleague Friedrich believes you are a deformed idea-crippler, not to mention a cold-hearted bastard.

IMMANUEL: Maybe he is your colleague. Did he call me a bastard? Then he is a selfish bastard, as far as I'm concerned, and his popularity proves my point. No matter what he thinks, duty is done only by those who act according to the rational authority of an impersonal moral imperative rather than pursuant to some private inclination of their own, including the barbaric lust of for power. Friedrich is irrational: he knows nothing of true virtue and thinks virtue lies in the will to power.

BARUCH: How can virtue be true and not exist? I think you have contradicted yourself. And what happened to saying of others what you would have them say of you? I would think you would appreciate the fact that he, like you, looked around and found no virtue in the world. Only his imaginary superman was capable of virtue.

IMMANUEL: Not Christian virtue, which requires a personal and humiliating crucifixion so the impersonal law can be fulfilled. God's law makes no exceptions for persons.

BARUCH: But God's love is in every person. The universal scheme is God's love expressed.

IMMANUEL: Spoken like a true pantheist. Of course a pantheist is nothing but an atheist. At least the youth corrupted by Friedrich loved a charismatic superman in lieu of God, while your narcissistic youth love only themselves, thinking God is within each person of the plurality.

BARUCH: You mistake me as far as things go. I do not love things as if the deity were in them.

IMMANUEL: But do you love the thing-in-itself?

BARUCH: What?

IMMANUEL: You know, the underlying thing, the unknown thing-in-itself, the Thingie.

BARUCH: Do I love the unknown? How would I know? I do know that daily life was so hollow and futile for me that I decided to discover whether or not the good life existed. By that I mean a life of continuous and supreme joy to all eternity. I found neither good nor evil in the things that I was anxious over. Along the way I discovered that self-esteem is the highest thing we can hope for.

IMMANUEL: There it is again – the Dear Self. And what is self-esteem?

BARUCH: Self-esteem is the joy of knowing one's power.

IMMANUEL: Good grief. Neither good nor evil without, but omnipotence within is the thing.

"Gentlemen," I interjected, "excuse me for interrupting, but may I say something? Harry Frankfurt, my professor of philosophy at Princeton, professed that there should be nothing shameful or unfortunate about our self-love, for we are told by an author of the greatest authority that we should love our neighbors as we love ourselves, therefore self-love is not an enemy of virtue at all, but is rather its prerequisite. The ardent manner in which we love ourselves is the best model for loving others, so let us love them as enthusiastically as we love ourselves. By self-love Professor Frankfurt did not mean self-indulgence, for to serve the best interest of another might require self-restrain: merely indulging him might not be in his best interest. Is not this the way to go?"

My question put an end to the séance; the spirits fled, leaving me alone with my own thoughts. If only Tracey had not gone off to find her soul, if she had fully understood that the material girl had become a spiritual girl because she had a soul in the first place, I thought, she would be with us today.

Tracey's Secret Source

"What are you doing up there, Walter?" Harriet yelled up to me as I carried a few things out of Tracey Flagler's apartment after her suicide. Harriet, a beautician and brazen hussy of sorts from Great Britain, lived in the apartment directly below, but she was seldom seen around the complex. Her brassy voice was occasionally heard by all from time to time as she conversed with one resident or another at the top of her lungs on the walkway, usually voicing complaints about the poor upkeep up the property.

"Tracey's stuff is up for grabs," I responded over the railing. "The landlord said we can take whatever we want before the Salvation Army truck gets here."

"I don't know if I could touch anything of hers. That woman was a weird witch. She was into the spirit world - I could tell that, I'm sensitive to that kind of thing... Oh, look at this crap!" she said, waving at the litter in the yard, and then pointing at the huge pile of dog excrement on the sidewalk outside her door. "These people are from the wrong side of the tracks. I try to keep the area in front of my apartment clean, but a lot of good that does with this kind of neighbor around. I called the landlord the other day. Why doesn't he clean this place up regularly, and paint the buildings, I asked him. 'Who would want to rent apartments in your dirty place?' I asked, and I told him I was so ashamed to have guests that I might move out any time now."

"I had the Queen Elizabeth over yesterday," I jested, "and she was appalled by the deplorable conditions here. Come on up, there's a big chair and a couch up here, maybe there's something you can use."

"I don't know. It's a bad thing what she did, doing herself in like that. She was a dope addict, I bet, and a slag."

"What is a slag?"

"A slag is a tawdry tart, but she doesn't bother to charge, just gives it away to everyone."

"You mean a slut? I saw only one boyfriend around"

"That black man was probably her pimp or dope connection, maybe both."

"So you think she was charging after all?"

"Well, I didn't know her, really. I suppose a girl has got to do what she has to do, but I didn't like her."

"Why didn't you like her?"

"I've got to get my sleep, you know, and that bitch was a noisy one, rattling the railing when she chained her bike, pacing around and around all night long up there like a crazy woman, and I could hear her bloody cats scrambling around on the floor all the time."

"Aw, Harriet, give her a break. We've got to make allowances for people. I think she was really a sweet girl. Come on up, see if there's anything you want."

Harriet climbed the flight of stairs and entered the apartment with me: "Whew! What a smell!"

"It's the cats, and the kitchen drain is clogged up with dead roaches."

"Gawd, look at this place! I knew it. I knew she was dirty bitch. I'm glad she's out of here, but I'm worried someone worse will move in, will be stomping around up here and disturbing me. I heard you walking around. I never make noise – do you hear my stereo playing downstairs?"

"No. But the ceilings are thin, and if the windows are open the neighbors can hear everything – the woman in the front building is a screamer, she keeps waking me up with her orgasms."

"Really, now, I've never seen her with anyone."

"I don't think she has a lover. She had her lamp on one night when she woke me up with her groans. I looked into her open window from mine and she was masturbating with a long purple dildo. So I wrote her a polite note about it and put it under her door. I offered to help her out with no strings attached. I enjoy being used to please a woman, and I need the practice, but I need my sleep, I wrote, and I myself would sleep better after a climax or two if I got to bed early. Now she keeps her back window closed and her curtain pulled."

"Hmm...that's very interesting. I might like to help her out myself, but I'm glad she doesn't live above me."

"Harriet, the noise wasn't Tracey's fault, really. This whole apartment complex is like an echo chamber. All you got to do is say boo to wake everyone up at night. Look how the floor buckles as we walk on it. Why don't you move into this room, be on top instead of below? Then you wouldn't be bothered by people and other animals walking around on your ceiling."

"Not after she's been here. This place can never be cleaned enough. I can feel something weird in here. I tell you, I can feel that sort of thing. Don't you feel it? She was weird, a voodoo woman, I'll bet. Look at that little string doll with stuff on it, hanging by the door there. And all that pacing – she must have been on heroin."

"No. Pacing would be speed or cocaine. Actually, I took her diaries after I found her corpse, and I found out she had kicked drugs. Alcohol was the big problem. Some people seem to be born into withdrawal. They want something to curb the inborn craving, to dampen the energy, or to help them just let go of it and do what it wants."

"Yeah, I know," Harriet said, with an understanding look.

"She craved power but she also wanted to totally relax, so the booze got her high and depressed her too."

"When you have total power you also totally relax because nothing stands in your way when it's uncorked," Harriet opined wittily.

"She was in AA, was dry for a long time, and getting herself together. That's why she rode her bike, and probably why she paced a lot, trying to outpace demon alcohol."

"Oh, poor thing," Harriet's whole demeanor had softened. I suspected she was an alcoholic herself, and had picked up her brazen attitude in London pubs. "I saw her on the beach in the mornings, doing yoga."

"Trying to calm down, get some peace. Her long hours as a waitress did not tire her out, as she was gripped by a terrible thirst for spirits"

"Oh, I understand, that's why she killed herself..."

"And when she was not pacing around, she was writing in circles in her notebooks, repeating herself over and over, drawing wheels with 'I' in the center of each one and writing wishes between the spokes. She often addressed an imaginary friend named Abraham in her notebooks, and referred to the Secret."

"Oh my God!" Harriet exclaimed. "She was into the Secret?"

"Yeah, she was. I hear lots and lots of people got into it since Oprah started recommending it. I feel sorry for Tracey. She got so deeply involved with the Secret cult, got her hopes raised sky high just to be let down, and then she felt guilty because the Secret had taught her that she was responsible for failure. I think that's part of what killed her. Someone ought to do a study of the relationship between suicide and the Secret."

"What are you saying? What's wrong with the Secret? The Secret is wonderful!"

"For one thing, as the real African high priest revealed to his initiate, there is no secret in the sacred lodge. Anyway, the whole thing about the Secret turned me off after I read the Salon's revelation of what is really going on with that."

"What salon gossip is that? What's the name of the salon?"

"Not a beauty salon, an Internet magazine called the Salon."

"What was said?"

"For one thing, the guy who wrote the article, Peter Birkenhead, thinks Oprah is ruining her reputation recommending the Secret. I got the impression that he thinks Oprah is a greedy bitch, to use your word."

"What a dickhead he is today that! Oprah is not a bitch and she would not recommend the Secret unless it was good."

"He says Oprah is preaching Golden Bull, the worship of Mammon and the love of money, and that the Secret is the usual instant-success, instant-gratification, self-help snake oil in a rosy bottle. If you drink a bottle every day, then you can lay your hands onto $2.5 billion like she did, just take a swig and visualize the bucks well enough and talk it up, and if you don't get it it's your own damn fault for making bad choices. She claims that the only reason any person does not have enough money is because they are blocking money from coming to them with their negative thoughts."

"She's right. Your thoughts set up magnetic waves that attract whatever you want."

"Do you have your million, yet, Harriet?" I asked with a smile.

"I'm working on it. I deserve one as must as anyone else. There's no reason why anyone doesn't have a million if they really want one and focus on it. You don't have to be a Jesus or Moses to be millionaires like they were."

"OK, you know the Secret. The Salon writer said if the secret of the Secret were true, then people deserve to get bad things because they have bad thoughts, that poor people deserve to be poor, people in Darfur deserve to be raped and murdered by the Janjaweed, stuff like that. If you don't get something good, too bad for you – I guess you kill yourself, maybe take a few people with you."

"That makes sense," Harriet claimed. "Losers block good stuff with wrong thinking. I don't want to do that. I want to be the best me I can be, a leader and not a follower!"

"You go girl! I can tell you that Tracey adored Oprah and even wanted to teach the Secret. Oprah has set herself up now as Secret teacher. What the guy at the Salon seems worried about is that the being all you can be in our culture amounts to being as greedy as you can be, grabbing everything you can for yourself. The faith of the Secret is placed in the self, in believing in the self whatever it might be instead of actually knowing the self including one's limits. Consumers who do not know themselves nor know what to do to be successful enough to buy whatever they think they might want instead of what they really need, flock to hear this magical means of instant success. In other words, Oprah is a cheesy con woman and the Secret is a cheap con."

"That's a lot of pong! Oprah's a goddess, the most honest woman in the world, and she didn't get rich conning people. We're not stupid! She knows how we feel, and we don't have to feel weird with her, like we're freaks because of sex, our looks, because we are overweight, did drugs. She's someone we can confess to and help ourselves. What does that bloody critic know about anything? He's a blooming idiot and they can shove him. I'll bet he's got a small one and can't make a living with his negative writing. You've got to think big, visualize what you want, that's what I say. Excuse me now, I've got to get back to the salon – I'm working twelve hours today."

"You work long hours."

"It's worth it. Beauty inspires."

"Don't you want any of Tracey's stuff? How about this stuffed chair?"

"No, it's too big. I have my own stuff. You know, I'm glad you told me about Tracey. There was something I always liked about her, but I didn't know what it was. If only she had kept on thinking about what she wanted, but in the right way, she would have gotten it and would be living joyfully now. I wish we had gotten together for tea while she was here. We would have been good friends, I'm sure. God bless her. May she rest in peace!"

Tracey's Madame Huong

Martin Berdinger is a certified public accountant and a lawyer and a professor of tax law, but he is more of an attorney than an accountant, and more of a professor than the foregoing. The professions of keeping accounts, telling tales, and professing laws are closely related at history's source, where bookkeepers tallied up goods for kings and pharaohs, went on to give accounts of events, and then professed to know how things should occur, turning to the people's side when disgruntled.

Accountants are not famous for their sense of humor or people skills; they usually do not have much to say and are focused more on the facts than are the lawyers who put the facts to trial. That is, lawyers are naturally more verbose by trade than accountants, and lawyers who win most often are certainly more persuasive than their opponents; they tell a good story when they present their client's case, supporting it the best they can with evidence and substantive and procedural law. To that end the lawyer must have a sense of humor, for his practice will eventually dispose him to cynicism, which is no enemy to comic irony; a sense of humor tends to disarm he who tries the facts. The imagination of good professors, even professors of tax law, extends beyond the facts and the law, for they would bring the light to the people, and that light, in the interest of some purportedly higher justice, might outshine the pharaoh and his magistrates, wherefore such public defenders have been called lucifers; i.e. "light-bearers." Yet no matter how far the imagination might fly into the abstract realm, we are stuck with figures of speech based on concrete experience.

My first impression of Professor Berdinger, who introduced himself to me with a private lecture on the "blessed federalism of percolating states," was that he was, notwithstanding his reputation as a tax wizard, somewhat of a crackpot, an impression augmented by the bloody bandage on his bald pate – the absentminded professor said he had been thinking of a States' Rights tax case when he arose from bed that morning and stumbled head first into the glass panels of his wife's antique china cabinet.

The reader may imagine what I thought of the professor when I became acquainted with his part in the scandal over the Miami Herald's so-called Death Tower, and when he handed me Madame Huong's card and told me to call on her, using the code name, General Peace, and said that the unwritten portion of my job description mandated that I help her market "happy hats." I considered begging askance of the partners at Landoro & Lawk at the time, but Professor Berdinger had been their consultant for many years and was highly esteemed by them, staid as they were, so I did not want to embarrass myself and risk my position by being out of order. And I was glad that I had desisted after I read a number of court opinions the professor had cited, for all of his definite positions seemed backed by judicial legislation, lowering my opinion of the Third Branch while raising my estimate of the professor's position on it. As for the Death Tower, there might be something to it as far as I knew. And as for Madame Huong, I supposed Professor Berdinger was playing a practical joke on me, so I decided to humor him and to call on her. As coincidence would have it, the famous artist and peace activist happened to be exhibiting a few million dollars of her artwork at South Beach's famous Washington Avenue and Lincoln Road. I researched her background before calling on her there.

If she only she had been born and raised in the United States, Nguyen Thi Thanh Huong would make a great poster child for the real violence Americans say they do not want children to witness at home although they allow the media to feed their kids a steady diet of violent images that induces many of them to engage not only in violence at home but in massively organized terrorism abroad to advance the American way of life their enemies are allegedly so jealous of. She was raised in Vietnam hence experienced firsthand the horrors of the American-led war on its communistically inclined peasantry. Indeed, her self-portrait is entitled Dead Dove: a crying girl holds dead bird. She graduated from Vanhanh University in 1972 with a degree in journalism, and reported on the daily atrocities of war; for example, she interviewed war widows who were giving their last ounce of flesh, prostituting their bodies to support their children. Her own family sided with the capitalists: She lost several members of her immediate family, including a brother who was killed and a brother who committed suicide, and her father died after being imprisoned by the communists for nine years – eventually, in 1992, the communist government of reunited Vietnam released eleven members of her family, with whom she was reunited in Washington, D.C.

Madame Huong jumped into a refugee boat with her baby son in her arms the day before South Vietnam fell – her son was destined to develop a computer animation business in America, which he sold for several million dollars after he turned 25. The overcrowded boat was refused landing in several Eastern countries, but American sailors rescued the refugees when the boat arrived in the Philippines. She wound up in a refugee camp in California, but soon ventured to Kodiak Island in hopes of securing a job at a canning factory, where English was not required for employment. That job did not work out, but she stayed in Alaska for 10 years, where she replaced her "broken" pen of journalism with a painter's brush, learning the artistic carving method of intaglio from the Native Americans with whom she traveled about at length - Eskimos and Vietnamese share a common, Mongolian ancestry. She produced lovely, optimistic works of art, representative of her uplifting experience in Alaska, where she also taught in a community college for some time.

And then the enterprising artist with son in tow traveled thousands of miles in a 1976 Buick station wagon in North America over a period of four years. She also plied her art in Central America, South America, and the Caribbean. She eventually settled in South Florida, opening her first gallery at Boca Raton's Wharfside shopping center. In 1992 she met Bank America executive and art collector Glen Ryals when he bought 'Moon Song', a portrait of two lovers among roses. He opened Ryals Gallery in 1993: "Opening the gallery was the only way he could keep me in town. Glenn is a very smart man." (Boca Raton News, April 24, 1998). They married in 1995, the same year the Vietnam and the United States governments re-established a formal relationship. The bride soon proceeded to paint 'The War Pieces', depicting her horrifying experiences in Vietnam. Her war art was mainly exhibited at the Art, War & Peace Museum in Jensen Beach. At the turn of the century, the couple took up residence in a Miami mansion they acquired and renovated, naming it the Art Palace.

My rich and famous friend Helene and I viewed a great deal of Madame Huong's art in the enormous space the peace artist had rented next to McDonald's on South Beach. Helene is of course an Neo-Impressionist of note who has served the world from time to time as an art curator, is presently an art advocate on various boards and councils, and she is a volunteer public relations consultant for charities dealing with spousal and child abuse as well – she was brutally beaten by her powerful husbands.

Madame Huong's peace exhibit did not appeal to me at first glance. I used to be a weekend hippie, and of course I am a freethinker, but at heart I am a conservative from the Heart of America. For one thing, I happen to know that war is what made America great, and that is why America's neoconservatives, whose elders attributed their political prejudice to Germany's New Conservatism until the death camps were exposed, tend to blame everything that is wrong with America on the [expletive deleted] pacifists. It is war that makes a man a man – without it he has no moral fiber worth speaking about. His woman should stand slightly behind him on his right side, gaze at him with admiring eyes, and pass him ammunition and cannon meat. The romance is in the war. Peace is generally viewed as obsolete except as a preparation to make war for another peaceful break for sexual intercourse to prepare for more peacemaking war in the name of the god of love. Moreover, the vestiges of the Peace Movement of the Sixties are dated and associated with recalcitrant hippies and other diehard weirdoes: The Vietnam War embarrassment was laid to rest under the glorious victory of the First Bush War on Iraq; American's regained the guts to stay the course when spreading their version of democracy abroad, just as they did in the World Wars, instead of turning tail when the going gets very bloody; wherefore they have given up mere police actions such as those pursued in Korea and Vietnam, and have taken up fighting the World War on Terrorism with a vengeance.

However than might be, the sight of so much crimson cubism clashing in one place at Madame Huong's South Beach exhibit overwhelmed the peace purportedly intended by her obvious overstatement of violence. My dear Helene, a military brat, neoconservative hawk, and fine friend to established right-wing authority, sympathized with my first impression. But Helene has what she calls "pink insides," which are attracted to the liberals she otherwise deplores. She has an eagle eye for fineries including the finest of fine art, and she is, in the final analysis and much to her credit, a just woman.

"You're right, it's overbearing, but only on the whole," she responded when I voiced my discomfited criticism. "Look at the Picasso designs, for example those pieces over there, one by one. They're brilliant. I think I might like to buy one for my Waldorf apartment, another for my Virginia home."

"Your Washington friends might be appalled by pacifist art."

"Not at all: they appreciate valuables no matter what the context might be."

"Madame Huong grew up in Vietnam," I offered. "Her family's home had a single one piece of art displayed, a copy of Picasso's The Three Musicians."

"You don't say. This one here reminds me of his Guernica. It is absolutely frightening. I would like to have it. I must have a word with her."

"Helene, it's all too depressing. See that woman raining tears of blood? How awful. You're around abused women and children too much in your charities – you need something optimistic. Take that one over there, the big one with the huge doves on it."

"Doves of peace," Helene remarked.

"The doves symbolize the white stars of the American flag – the red is also from the flag, and stands for the blood of millions of people spilled. The doves want peace in Iraq."

"The violent paintings are the best," Helene observed.

"Violence begets violence. It's as if victims are attracted to their abusers. Madame Huong said that great art comes from great sorrow. Her whole country was abused."

"She's right about great art, but please don't criticize the war, my father was doing the right thing."

"She's obviously cashing in on abuse big time," I went on, at risk of getting her gal. "War is the worst abuse of all, and now that it's politically incorrect to chastise women and children at home, men have to rely on war even more to let off steam. Why don't you ask Madame Huong about her earlier paintings, the optimistic ones she did before she felt compelled to confront her violent past and express her horror with war. "

"I smell money," Helene sniffed. "I know these Vietnamese – they look out for themselves, and are keen to make a profit. I shall buy something from her."

"I think you should get away from the violence in the name of peace, Helene. Don't be a masochist."

"Stop it, Walter, you're upsetting me. No man is going to tell me what to do, you know that."

"Excuse me, let's not fight."

"I know what I want, Walter. You seem to know a lot about her. She's up to something."

"I was referred to her at work, so I looked into her background."

"Oh, did you, now? May I tell you what people should say when you say you will look into something?"

"What's that?"

"They should say, Please don't."

"Why is that?"

"You are like a dog on a bone once you take up a subject – you dig up skeletons in the basement. .... Hmm, her work looks carved – she's good with palette knife, and she cuts her lines with something, probably the other end of her brush. And see how she throws her paint? Ah, the paint looks cracked, she's heated it, and there's a grainy texture."

"Her line is great," I added. "I was impressed by her line and when I saw black-and-white photocopies of her compositions. But the color is outlandish. There is too much red, too much blood. It's all too shocking, too garish for me. I'm sick and tired of the violence – I want peace now."

"I thought liberals liked red," Helene teased.

"I'm not a communist."

"Maybe she is. Maybe she's a spy. She cut up an American flag."

"She hates communists, Helene."

"You have said yourself that God loves Satan because God needs a devil in order to be God."

"I'm going to interview her for my living novel about Tracey Flagler."

"What about your living novel about me? Why don't you put her in my novel?"

"Don't worry, Helene, there will be more about you, something sexy too."

"Don't upset me. And stop looking at my breasts. She's coming our way."

Happy Hats

"Madame Huong, my name is Paul Bowman, and this is my good friend, Helene Fulsome."

"Pleased to meet you," Madame Huong said, her face beaming. "Thank you for coming to our peace exhibit. Would you like some Russian tea?"

"That would be nice," Helene accepted.

"Mary, bring some tea for our guests," Madame Huong directed a member of her staff. "Are you here for the peace meeting?"

"Well, no, we are appreciating your art," declared Helene.

"We must appreciate peace."

"It's very sad, really."

"And beautiful," Helene added.

"Art happens when your tears connect with my tears."

"I was recommended to you by Martin Berdinger," I explained. "He said to mention general peace and happy hats, so I thought I would drop by your opening."

"Martin! He is a good lawyer – he helped me with my estate planning."

"Excuse me," Helene said, "I'm going to walk around a little more, and enjoy your art."

"We are having a peace meeting here, at eight. We can stop the violence, and we must stop it so we can live in peace and harmony."

"We did not know about the meeting, and have made other plans," I said, noting to myself that anti-war peace was obviously out of vogue, a least in hedonistic South Beach – the exhibit hall was deserted.

"We must plan for peace," Madame Huong persisted. "We must unite in peace and harmony."

"May I call on you tomorrow?" Helene asked. "I believe we may agree on one or two of your works."

"Of course – I will busy at the peace demonstration on Lincoln Road until four, so come after five."

"Good. I'm going to look around, Paul, do take your time." Helene sauntered off.

"Madame, how much is the art here worth? My guess is five million."

"Your guess is good. Five million is the insured value," she responded. "But we are not here for money. We are here for peace."

"But of course," I agreed and nodded at the suited fellow at a computer behind a counter adorned with VISA and MASTERCARD 'Accepted Here' signs. "But sometimes we must make war to defend ourselves. Even Mahatma Gandhi agreed with that.

"Why war? War produces nothing. We must not fight each other. We must fight for unity. We must fight for peace. We must fight violence. We must fight our vices and weaknesses."

There it is again, I thought, the ubiquitous word, "fight." There always has to be a fight instead of a persuasion or conversion. The hundreds of millions of war dead prove that there are all sorts of unities to fight for, and that not even a world war to end all wars can end wars. The other side of unity is division, and without division there is no such thing as unity except in Nothing.

"Who is going to protect peaceful people like you, Madame, from rapists, murderers and thieves? Evil is multiplying in your world today. The police and soldiers protect you. Someone wants to break into your gallery, steal your art, and rape and kill you if you are there. Maybe someone just hates the peace movement, or enjoys hurting people. But the police protect you. The police and soldiers must guard the peaceful ones as the circle widens, until everyone drinks of the loving cup. They might have to kill people to defend you, to support your peace movement."

"Soldiers and police come to see me and they go in peace. Man has a good heart. All people really want peace. If given a choice between war and peace, people will choose peace."

"But Madame, history proves that people choose war because they love violence."

"We must fight our weakness. We must fight against war."

"But how can you fight war without war?"

"Just say no to war. Just stop the violence. Just stop it, that's all. We can just stop the violence. Think peace. Everybody must think peace. There will be peace."

"Your art is amazing, Madame. Still, the war pieces are very depressing, and drown the peace pieces in an ocean of blood. But maybe it's good to remember the violence, just like the Jews remember the holocaust, so people will want the opposite, and not deny the horror and bring it about again, thinking such things can never happen."

"The holocaust was a long time ago," Madame Huong retorted dismissively – I detected a jealous twinge in her tone. The Jews keep talking about the holocaust. They must get over it. We must come together under one tent and forget the Jews and separations. We must think about the future. We must think peace."

"The Vietnam War has also been over a long time. I guess you are just sick and tired of hearing about the white man's holocaust – he doesn't care about Asians. Still, I wonder if it does any good to show violent images no matter what they are about. I think people get sexually and violently aroused by pornography and violent images."

"It's not the violence I hold up. I hold up the nobility. I hold up the noble faces of the victims looking up at the sky in pain and crying blood. I see myself in their faces."

"You are noble," I tried to flatter her.

"Not just me. Everybody is noble. We must all get together, come to meetings, and think peace and act for peace. We must end the separations and hatred. Here, take this," she ordered, holding out a black Magic Marker. "Now write something on this painting. Don't worry. Go ahead. Write something, whatever comes to mind."

I was at a loss for words, but finally scrawled, "I am sick of war."

"You must sign it."

I spontaneously signed, 'General Peace.'

"There, now, your name is General Peace."

"Professor Berdinger said you had happy hats to market. What are they?"

"He means our peace helmets. General Peace of the World Peace Force needs peace helmets so his troops will be protected from bad vibrations. They can tune into peace and make themselves happy. We have developed a prototype. Mary," she called to her assistant, "please take General Peace to the dressing room and show him our happy hat."

"So you are General Peace." Mary sang matter-of-factly as she led me to a back room. The buxom, long-haired young woman was wearing a pink T-shirt upon which an image of a large peace sign made of hemp was emblazoned; her designer tennis shoes and low-cut jeans were fashioned with a raggedy look; she wore no makeup and smelled of Ivory soap. I got the impression from her confident bearing and gait that she was a professional woman who dressed-down, like a hippie, to suit peace demonstrations. Her hips fascinated me inordinately, having a hypnotic effect as her rear swayed from side to side like a pear on a pendulum as I followed her down a long hall to the rear of the building. I was feeling slightly ecstatic, and wondered if the Russian tea had been spiked with something. She entered a combination on a keypad by the door at the end of the hall, and gestured into a room awash in pink light.

"Come in," she beckoned. "Please sit down. Good." She extracted a key hidden deep in the valley of her bosom and used it to unlock a shiny hatbox, apparently made of black plastic, sitting on the table. She took out a rainbow-hued, diamond-like helmet and handed it to me. It appeared to be made of a brilliant, translucent crystalline substance, veined with thin silver wires. I examined it closely: the crystals were tetrahedrons.

"The red is dead, the rainbow is rising, let there be peace and prosperity in the world," Mary sang. "Here, let me put it on you," she said, and leaned over me. There was something very appealing about her. She was short of stature, and when she approached me to put the helmet on my head, I felt tempted to bury my face in her T-shirted bosom, put my arms around her, grab her bottom and give her a hug.

"I know what you're thinking. Don't worry, that's how people feel about you after you wear the Peace Helmet There, now" she placed the helmet on my head. "That's it. Enjoy. The red is dead, the rainbow is rising. Be happy."

"O my god, oh, uh, ah...."

"What does it feel like, General Peace? Do you feel good?"

"Oh, yes, yes, it feels like, it feels like I'm going to, I mean...."

"Like an orgasm, like your whole body is going to cum?"

"Yes, yes, oh yes!"

"Yes, relieve yourself of yourself. Let yourself go. The rainbow is rising."

"Oh, man, I feel so good," I moaned. I was in a state of continuous relief, of perpetual peace, if you will, and everything was crystal clear. Mary had levitated: she was hovering slightly above me, basking in an aura of multi-colored light. I noticed that she had no navel but thought nothing of it. Indeed, as I let myself go, or came, so to speak, it was as if I was some other I, as if someone were thinking and feeling for me, playing my body like a musical instrument.

"General Peace," Mary proceeded with a singsong, "People shall assemble throughout the world as one in many to invoke your peace. They shall call upon you to lead them on the way to supreme peace, and you shall come, and your mouth shall speak glad tidings, your hand shall write good news, and your feet shall bring peace upon Earth. The peoples shall cry with joy, for sorrow and sadness shall be nevermore, and joy and gladness shall be evermore. The nations shall recognize their wrongs and come unto you for peace. Their leaders shall close their mouths and open their ears, and you shall fill their minds and hearts with eternal peace. Tyrants shall hang on your every word, lay down their weapons and have them destroyed or converted to peaceful uses. Earth shall be perfected and shall serve up her abundance according to the generosity of every one towards every other."

"Earth shall be perfected and shall serve up her abundance according to the generosity of every one towards every other." I repeated spontaneously.

"Hunger and disease shall be no more, and the desire for joy, peace, love, and eternal life shall be satisfied in mutual service."

"Hunger and disease shall be no more, and the desire for joy, peace, love, and eternal life shall be satisfied..." I reiterated.

"You are General Peace."

"You are General Peace."

"No, you are General Peace."

"I am General Peace."

"Yes. You shall marshal the forces of peace and lead the lords of liberation with words of power from the source of oneness. You shall focus consciousness on peace and love. You shall make the Unknown One known. You shall command the reconstruction company, and the world shall be home again to the homeless. Say this: I shall make the world home again to the homeless"

"I shall make the world home again to the homeless."

"Say I feel the joy of service, and I am crystal clear."

"I feel the joy of service, and I am crystal clear."

"Joy is in service, not in selfishness."

"Joy is in service, not in selfishness."

"The red is dead, the rainbow is rising."

"The rainbow is rising."

"All right, General Peace," Mary confirmed, alighted on the floor and took the helmet from my head – it was glowing with color, as if a prism had cast spectral rays upon it – and put it back in the gleaming black hatbox.

"What happened? Everything was so clear, but what was it that you were saying?" I started slipping out of crystal clarity into the usual confused consciousness.

"You were happy. You will remember everything soon enough, offer it to the world, and the words of power will have good effects."

"It should be a bestseller. I remember feeling very good. I remember the rainbow, and you seemed to be floating towards the ceiling. I don't believe I ever felt so good. I still feel good, joyful, and very peaceful."

"The feeling will last for a few days. But please keep quiet about this until the marketing campaign begins."

"That's a real happy hat you've got there, lady."

Tracey's Channeling

"I'm thinking of how my life is perfect in terms of the progression of things," Tracey Flagler had confessed in her diary shortly before she took her life. "Fear and therapy got me in touch with my emotional guidance system even thought I could not apply it like you taught me, Abraham. And then came Seth, Ray, and Immanuel, and my heart totally opening, learning how to focus on choosing love, having a visceral, cellular experience for years, of being a blended being, and finding Immanuel stuff and Seth stuff and believing that I could create anything I want while wanting only joy along the way. Abraham, you are the best. I could learn to channel you really well in another five years, and find true love, money, joyful focusing, all the stuff we will finally get when we die because we want it, but I want it all now. Tell me, Abraham, can I get it now?"

Yes O Shaloma If You Focus On Joy Create The Right Vibrational Field You Will Become Shaloma Magneta And Attract The Things You Desire.

"But why couldn't my relationship with Peter just be easy? I focused on joy and I vibrated the best I could. I wanted it to be easy. I wanted a relationship where it is so natural and so right that we wouldn't question it even if it is challenging and there is asking going on. Why couldn't it be about fun and more fun, or joy and more joy? It should have been so easy. Men are so stupid! Why couldn't he believe it was worth any challenge for the joy being together brings?

Relationships are so stupid. I am so stupid. I want to be a vibrational match. But I don't feel like my life counts like a life should. I feel like if I had a family I would feel secure like there was more of a reason to focus and feel joy. But my vibrations don't work that way. Why? The Law of Attraction brings me stupid men. I am a stupid magnet, so stupid that I attract stupid ones. I get my hopes up for fun and joy, attract some stupid man, and then I get shot down because I'm stupid. I don't know what it is in my vibration that says I need to be alone, that attracts men only to make them run away from me. Maybe it is just stupidity."

They Leave Only Because They Don't Have A Positive Focus You Like That And So Do They And Like Attracts Like.

"I seem to attract the opposite of what I like."

There Is No Effect Without A Cause O Dear One You Unconsciously Want What You Consciously Think You Don't Want And Everything Falls Into Its Proper Place But Do Not Blame Yourself O Shaloma Know This You Are Evolving And Better Is Coming You Are Doing An Excellent Job Evolving To The Lowest Energy Stabilization Where You Can Completely Relax And Enjoy Yourelf Remember The Secret You Are Immortal You Can Create Your Own Reality Continue To Use The Law Of Attraction To Play The Field And Attract A Lover He Will Be Wealthy And You Will Be Rich And Famous People Will Love You On The Oprah Show Remember O Dear One You Are Amazing.

"But I want to be so okay that I would be fine if I never had a partner or lover. I would still feel satisfied and fulfilled without one. What's the use of trying to attract what does not exist? I was lying in bed and was feeling how a relationship would help me to open up and relax and connect with the source. But no one is trying to see what an amazing person I am. They are all trying to look out for themselves and feel amazing themselves! So I am alone. When I put that into the context of eternity, I will never fit in: I will die without a mate and a house and a career. I will never become a famous channel and get on the Oprah show. I will be alone forever, with nothing to do. I will be dead."

O Dear One You Cannot Die You Shall At Least Be In Eternity And That Is Enough But You Can Be More Than That You Can Be Much More Connected To The Source If You Focus On Joy And Confidence And Eagerness And Wellness Use Your Vibrations To Create A Relaxing Magnetic Field You Can Create That Structure Of Being Smooth Out Your Waves And Make Them Longer And Circle The Earth Your Lover Will Find Your Hole And Fill It He Will Speed To You From Afar You Dear Shaloma Can Be Shaloma Magneta You Can Create A Vibratonal Structure Of Joy Anytime Just Relax Into That Structure And Feel The Flow Of Energy Let Joy Be Your Lover. Just Say Yes To Love And Love Yourself And You Shall Be Loved Because Love Feels Good And Love Is Joy And Your Mission O Shaloma Is To Joyously Choose Thoughts Words Actions That Feel Good While You Choose Them.

Of course I had heard of mediums before I retrieved and began reading Tracey Flagler's diaries and notebooks shortly after she departed to the Other Side. I did not know that the process had been renamed "channeling", nor did I know that mediating psychic entities is enormously popular nowadays, thanks in part to the revelations of such public figures as Oprah Winfrey, currently the high priestess of the New Age.

Oprah's guest, Shirley MacLaine, whose looks I liked at the time and whose professional role-playing I enjoyed, grew rich and famous consorting with channelers. They put her into touch with such prehistoric spirits as Cro-Magnon warrior Ramtha, but I did not take her role as a professional spiritual advisor seriously enough to pay much attention to her bizarre performances in that capacity. MacLaine apparently hailed from the lost continent of Atlantis, went looking for flying saucers, and flew beyond the Moon in Peru: No doubt she took some pretty good trips, but quite a few people were tripping in those days and some of them had far more interesting things to say. She chanted "I am God, I am God, I am God" and then hawked the usual New Age message: Dead people are not really dead. Everyone creates her own truths, realities and fates. Terrible consequences should not be condemned no matter how evil they might seem to be, for everything has a purpose and good and evil are merely relative if they exist at all.

A Christian spiritist may rightfully claim to channel Jesus if he sticks to scripture. But the New Age message does not match the faith in the one and only God, who appeared as his one and only Son, who is definitely not merely any and every man or woman who chants "I am God" or "I am Jesus." Such delusory beliefs as "I am Napoleon" or "I am Caesar" and so on are a sure sign of insanity.

Paranoia - delusions of persecution and grandeur – is indeed a ubiquitous symptom of our individualistic and discontented civilization, which has been uprooted from its traditional foundation in the spiritual monopoly established by Saul of Tarsus in the name of Jesus. He appeared in troubled times along with countless would-be messiahs, wandering faith healers, false prophets, pessimistic prognosticators, foolish soothsayers, vain self-exalters and the like. His purported mission was to restore order by establishing a universal religious monopoly under a divine monarch.

Jesus, the son of man, for what that's worth, was purportedly the Son of God as well, the one and only channel for God. It was God who filled him with the Holy Ghost that served him as his ghostly Spirit Guide. Jesus channeled tradition biblical entities: for example, on one haunted day Moses and Elijah appeared in their glory and palavered with him. Jesus traversed the Holy Land, healing the sick and raising the dead; but above all he cast out the competition, the demons and unclean spirits who served God's archangelic enemy, Satan, who was thrown out of heaven because he loved God so much that he hated man. Only those who cast out demons in Jesus' name were sanctioned by God, for they were not against him. But he advised his disciples not to rejoice in the subjection of spirits in his name, but to rejoice when they were worthy of having their names recorded in heaven.

One might say that only ministers who serve as mediums for Jesus and his heavenly father are true. And woe unto the hypocritical sophists and lawyers of the wicked generations who twist and spin the truth to exalt themselves and their wealthy clients; woe unto those who support the temples but have no love for the Lord. For those who exalt themselves shall be eventually humiliated and the lowly shall be raised high.

Jesus was no millionaire preacher of personal prosperity. Salvation seekers will be provided with as much as they need and nothing more: a loaf of bread, a cup of water, perchance some wine, and shelter for the night shall suffice, although man does not live by bread alone. Indeed, he urged his followers to abandon their selfish pursuits and to donate their goods to charity. Thus committed to charity, everything given shall be returned measure for measure, according to one's own standard of measure. Jesus did not appear on this planet to sell success books and seminars and to get rich quick: He appeared as a sign of Jonah, to warn the people of the doom awaiting them if they did not repent of their selfish ways – of course Jesus was far more ready to give the warning than Jonah, who, after the Lord had mercy on the repentant evildoers, may have been sick and tired of being made a fool of; or perhaps he thought they should not have gotten off so easy and wanted no part in making things easy for them.

As for personal salvation, Jesus did not say that people should love themselves and declare themselves gods. Someone asked: What shall I do to have eternal life? "You shall love the Lord your God with all your heart," Jesus declared, "and with all your soul, and with all your strength, and with all your mind; and your neighbor as yourself. Do this and you will live."

It is no wonder that unwholesome spirits writhe, moan and groan at the mention of the name of Jesus the Christ to this very day: "You are the Son of God!" they screamed when he laid his hands on the sick to heal them, but the son of man rebuked them and shut them up instead of making them whole. Was it because they dared to make a god out of a man? That would be a capital crime, no doubt unforgivable if the healing were worked on the Sabbath.

The New Age is utterly anti-Christian, despite giving occasional lip service to Christ. The most devout adherents to diverse and sundry postmodern cults tend to tolerate any sort of cult but Judeo-Christianity – if there must be a Christ, let him be not a Jew but a Greek or a Hindu. Secular Christianity's By-Goddery or bigotry, its often ruthless attempt to establish a monopoly over the souls of human beings and to distribute the absolute power worshipped is deeply resented. We cannot know if the world would have been better off without it. A postmodern reversion to hedonistic heathenism, pantheism, atheism and paganism proves nothing; it does not liberate humankind from its slavishness, and is likely to spurn the saints and elect a demonic man to madden and stampede the crowd over the cliff. Jews deny that Jesus is their expected Messiah, and the iconoclastic-minded among them eschew the worship of any man-god. Religion constitutes the worship of absolutely infinite power, which is unlimited by any form, including the mere image of the Lord. One may wonder how faith in such a god differs from nothing at all, or Nothing, but at least one can say that such a faith, unlimited by nature's conditions, including one's own faults, is ultimately conducive to liberty. It is this unconditional freedom from the world and its diverse material things and psychic entities that spiritual monopolists in truth sell. "Give me liberty or give me death," finds unmitigated liberty in death and rebirth into eternity, where Nothing or God exists.

Tracey Flagler finally has the relaxation she craved, may she rest in peace. A psychic entity counseled her to throw down her life in return for glorious dominion over the world. She took the test: She took her life into her own hands and ended it, and now she is in the hands of her maker, so to speak, in timeless eternity.

Tracey Flagler appeared as a sign, as a red flag, and the ever so slight trace of her existence in space-time cannot be erased. The fact that she existed at all shall persevere forever, despite her death. Whether anyone shall remember her a generation hence remains to be seen. Since the day I found her bare body, so cold, pale and fair, stretched out on her bloodstained bed, I have been stirred to speak of her predestined plight and her fatal flight therefrom.

Tracey Flagler's Sulfur-Fried Chicken

Having read over a dozen notebooks filled with Tracey Flagler's most intimate thoughts, I failed to fathom why such a vibrant and attractive young woman, who enjoyed sex immensely and whose sole aim in life was to experience and give joy, failed to attract a loving mate, and a small fortune besides, by virtue of the vibrations she had so diligently transmitted to that end. And in the end she took her own life, leaving me to find her remains, posed on her bloodstained, Sealy Posturepedic mattress in such a manner that I believed her delicious corpus was some sort of lesson that I was supposed to transmit to the world at large in the form of this living novel.

Tracey was possessed by the postmodern success culture: her enthusiasm was nearly unremitting: She read every issue of Oprah's magazine and watched the Oprah Winfrey show regularly and she read the transcripts of the shows she had missed in order to attune herself with celebrated success; she reiterated her positive affirmations to the point of psychopathological perseveration; she opened up psychic channels and received the advice of Abraham-Hicks, Immanuel, Seth and the like; every day she practiced sending out psychic pulses defined by the forceful but gentle repetition of the word love – love, love, love, love, love, love, love....

Alas, her faithful practice over several years was to little or no avail; in fact she had been rudely treated from time to time, or, even worse, completely ignored, yet, she continued to admire celebrities and did her best to love herself and others. Of course there were a few angry entries expressing her frustration over the fact she had not found a "vibrational match," that people "just don't get it, don't receive the vibrations." "I am feeling freaking frigging angry that people don't know that good feels good."

The psychic entities Tracey projected and served as medium for eventually "pissed" her off with their false prophesying. On rare occasions she railed against them out of sheer exasperation: "I hate you Abraham, I hate you Immanuel, I hate you Seth. Oh, how I hate all of you!" But for the most part she did not seem to have a mean bone in her body; the little one she did have turned the anger against the rest, and she killed herself instead of assassinating one or more of celebrities and psychic entities she catered to; the former in posh restaurants as a waitress, and the latter as a psychic medium. Why did the positive vibrations and the pop psychology of success espoused by movie stars and endorsed and advertised by her high priestess, the fabulously wealthy, former underdog, Oprah Winfrey, fail her? How did she fall out of sync? Why did her good vibes go awry? Why did her pursuit of happiness fall so pathetically short? After all, all the poor girl wanted was to have was fun and joy – money was merely the means. Good grief, what's wrong with that?

"I don't know why," she wrote in her last notebook, "but I have been feeling depressed for the last few days though everything has been going well. I have told myself over and over how much I appreciate my life, but now I feel really let down. I couldn't even stand the sight of Oprah on TV this afternoon – she looked as ugly as an ogre. I feel nauseated and confused. I have this weird taste, like sulfur, like I have matches in my mouth, and I feel like fried chicken. What's wrong with me? I feel terrified, I want to SCREAM and run away, but I can't get up and run, I can only write this, to try to stay in control. Abraham, did you lie to me? Where are you now? Why don't you answer me? I can't hear you inside my head. I heard noise, a whishing sound, a lot of static, and now I hear pounding and feel like a big hammer is banging me on my head. I am panicking, but I don't know where to go! Something is interfering with my vibrations. Oh, Abraham! What is this? What is happening to me? I think I'm going crazy! I don't know what I'm going to do!"

I showed Tracey's frantic scrawl to Martin Berdinger at Landoro & Lawk, the staid DWNTWN Miami accounting firm where I had uncannily obtained a position a few days after I discovered Tracey's body. By the way, the cabal that presides over Magic City caused downtown Miami to be officially dubbed 'DWNTWN', no doubt in consonance with the Cuban Hebrew clique of the highest rank.

I had placed a 50 word job-wanted ad on the Internet over an assumed name. I was called in for a one-hour interview, and I apparently landed the position because I'd sent out vibes while on the bus as it crossed the Mac Arthur Causeway, from South Beach to DWNTWN – perhaps I shall also find the million dollars I vibrated for to give good causes in the very near future. Quite a few bus riders read sacred texts or self-help maxim books, pray or chant mantras as the bus sails into Miami over the causeway. I, for one, am not religious or superstitious, so I switch on the diamond crystal, two-way radio the Dalai Lama psychically implanted in my third eye during his 2004 Hurricane Season visit to South Florida, to transmit my vibes.

Martin Berdinger was professor of tax law at Florida International University for a decade before he joined Landoro & Lawk, a firm famed for its decorum. The Professor, as he is affectionately called, is a wizard of sorts, sober-minded and levelheaded as can be when it comes to interpreting the Internal Revenue Code, a thoroughly underlined, dog-eared paperback copy of which he carries with him everywhere, perusing it while listening to Baroque adagios on his headphones; despite the staidness of the Firm, he certainly is not lacking in the imagination department.

Small in stature, he was a towering question mark to his students, constantly asking the hard questions, and demanding the right answers of them, or else. He whetted the appetite of the rebellious-minded among them by suggesting that individuals as citizens of the several states have certain inalienable rights as against the federal taxing authority, a scheme he referred to as "blessed federalism."

The Professor failed those students who did not dispute the Code; indeed, he approved of the ancient Jewish practice of whipping students who did not question the Torah. His inquisitive students soon learned that the federal government is actually supreme in its uniform imposition of the federal income tax laws on the citizens according to their graduated economic ranks; about the only inalienable right the taxpayer has is to comply voluntarily with the Code, regardless of what state she resides in. Other than complying with whatever is mandatory, citizens as well as states do have the right to do what is not expressly prohibited short of tort or breach of contract, and the legislature does its best to eliminate free-floating confusion in that regard by proliferating laws to fill the void; eventually nothing shall be allowed that is not pre-ordained; at least nothing untoward, i.e. nothing "unproductive" shall be permitted instead of the nihilist's everything.

Still, the citizen will feel that she has a free will, just as the brain-implant subject in Jose Delgado's experiment insisted that he was voluntarily turning his head to the left and right when his brain was remotely stimulated by the implanted stimoceiver: "I am looking for my slippers," he said. Moreover, since the citizen's behavior is determined, as if it were designed to obtain an end, she shall appear to be behaving rationally, just as Huxley's decapitated frog exhibited rational behavior.

The danger of becoming automatons, if not zombies programmed to "think" they are conscious, did not discourage the disaffected youth among the Professor's classes, for by the time they discovered the truth about centralized federalism within the answers to the questions the Professor had posed, they were, under his clever guidance, persuaded that the System was even more blessed than he had originally put it. He had, in effect, subtly enrolled them in the Master Tax Game, a system of mass behavioral manipulation through a process of conflict resolution that brings individuals and their groups into vertiginous harmony under the omniscient eye at the vertex of the political-economic pyramid scheme.

The Professor's most advanced students attended his biweekly séances, where brainwave-entrainment methods and subliminal suggestive-accelerative learning techniques were employed to regularly commit the principles and rules and most complex aspects of the Master Tax Game, including the latest tax angles, to memory for instant recall and appropriate application where needed. A few students used the technique to memorize the entire Code on their own, and to recall pertinent sections on demand using these techniques, but the Professor eschewed absolute rote memorization of Code and Regulation content, not to mention mere Opinions and Letters, fearing that it would turn tax practitioners into complete half-wits.

Professor Berdinger's favorite pastimes are calculus and writing. His most recent tomes, *Degrees of Judicial Certainty*, and *Calculating the Chance of Being Audited*, are available somewhere. He is naturally conservative. Pluralism he tolerates provided every governing authority embraces certain goods that are in some part common to the universal standard; namely, the Good. Disharmony or dissonance he abhors. The human being is naturally evil, he owns, for wherever some idea of good can be found, its opposite lurks nearby, rooted, as it were, in human nature. Therefore the Professor does not expect a political regimen to cure discontented individuals of their ills. Still, the Master Tax Game, at least as he conceives it, serves to tame the wild man within, who would quite naturally run amok without it, somewhere beyond good and evil like the horned god of absolute freedom, and brings him into calm concord with the good that evil tends to avoid or even evade if necessary.

FIU defrocked Professor Berdinger after he betrayed the Company with the Internet publication of a contumacious tome entitled 'The Herald Death Tower.' He referred to the tower that stands in the water near the Miami Herald building, which is positioned between the mainland ends of the Mac Arthur Causeway and Venetian Drive. The tower, he said, is known by Company operatives at the Herald's Hispanic sister-paper as El Torre de Muerte. Its objective, he claimed, was nothing less than inducing the outraged hysteria of the populace of Cuba through the remote transmission of extremely low frequency (ELF) waves, which Cubans would experience as sledgehammers, wielded by Fidel Castro, of course, smashing into their skulls. The chaos during the final, revolutionary broadcast would of course result in the overthrow of the Castro regime – rectifying helmets would supposedly be donned by insurgent leaders to protect them from the final pounding.

The so-called Torre de Muerte is allegedly being used in conjunction with a virtual mirror, an enormously long antenna in the ionosphere established by beaming microwaves from an array of antennas strategically dispersed on the Earth's surface. The Professor alleged that the Herald's Death Tower produces a secondary electromagnetic pool of radio waves around the tower, inducing all sorts of adverse emotional and physical effects in the vicinity, which, incidentally, has the highest rate of mental illness in the country, and is, according to a noted politician, so backwards that it is the only Third World city within the United States. Instead of shutting down the anti-Castro tower project, a decision was made to use the secondary electromagnetic field to make guinea pigs out of certain, suitably predisposed members of the population around the tower. A study of the Venetian Isles conducted by the Professor's students tallied all sorts of bizarre if not drunken and dope-crazed behavior, from mooning tourists as they sailed by aboard a sham pirate ship on the waterway, to assassinating joint-smoking celebrities. Incidentally, the Venetian Isles has the highest rate of dropped calls in the nation; the telecommunication companies know why, alleged the Professor, but mum is the word. Among the symptoms reported: exhaustion; pounding migraine headaches; accelerated heart beat; panic; vertigo; anger; depression; denial; auditory and optical hallucinations; the taste of sulfur; and generally feeling like a fried chicken.

Now it was the taste-of-sulfur and fried-chicken symptoms that raised my eyebrows when I read the Professor's paper after joining sedate Landoro & Lawk, where, to avoid diminishing the firm's reputation for sober-minded staidness with his scandalous past, the elf-like Professor keeps a very low profile in a huge comfortable chair, billing the partners a meager $150 per hour for his advice, which is amply supported by legal citations and Talmudic-like notes, some of them running into a dozens of pages. He insists that the law is "crystal clear" if read like a pyramid, taking every clause below in context of the headings above. He is always as certain as a neoconservative of the right thing to do in a particular case: "What must be done or not done in this situation is crystal clear," he says. There is no better person for an honest person to turn to for harmonious tax advice.

And perhaps the same might be truly said for sulfur and fried chicken, I surmised after I read the Professor's exposé on the Herald Death Tower, for a wise man or wizard, as Aristotle pointed out, is wise about many things in general, although he might not know how to make bread and butter.

My dear friend Helene, by the way, had tasted sulfur and felt like fried chicken, and she became deeply depressed and subject to panic attacks while living on the Venetian Isles. After being the subject of one of the worst runs of bad luck I have ever seen short of catastrophic death, including totaling a lawyer's car, she moved back to South Beach, where her health and her luck is slowly improving after she nearly died from a common cold and was conned into working for nothing for a mortgage foreclosure wheeler dealer. And, as mentioned, most recently the late Tracey Flagler, my erstwhile next door neighbor, had mentioned sulfur and fried chicken and the like in her complaints before she killed herself.

"It's crystal clear to me," said the Professor after reading Tracey's panicky note, "from the phenomena she describes here, especially the sulfur-fried-chicken effect, that your neighbor was affected by secondary transmissions from the Herald Death Tower."

"But why wasn't I affected?"

"You very well may be affected, but you simply don't know it yet. Everyone around here is affected in one way or another."

"Why don't they move away?"

"People who are not afraid of hurricanes and the fact that South Florida will soon be under water as Mr. Gore prophesied could care less about radio-wave poisoning. Mind you that some people are more sensitive to the transmissions than others. It appears from this note that your neighbor was pre-attuned and was a medium for Abraham."

"You know Abraham? He seems to be an imaginary friend of the New Age people."

"Abraham is a fictitious entity broadcast by the Company."

"Really?"

"Really."

"What do you mean by pre-attuned?"

"Was a micro-implant found in your neighbor – what was her name?"

"Tracey. Tracey Flagler."

"She allegedly committed suicide?"

"Yes."

"Did the autopsy uncover an implant?"

"I don't know anything about an autopsy."

"Probably nothing was found – the micro-implants are easy to insert without the subject knowing it, and are very difficult to detect unless you know what you're looking for."

"I don't believe in alien abductions, Professor."

"They are not alien deductions. Kid, you ain't in Kansas anymore."

"Maybe I ought to go back there before I turn in to a sulfur-fried chicken. Maybe everyone ought to get out of Dodge if what you revealed about the tower is true. Isn't everyone in Miami in danger? Why doesn't someone blow it up?"

"The tower itself is built to withstand hurricanes, and the generator is housed in a bomb-proof bunker. Anyone approaching the facility without a happy hat would be disabled, and someone wearing a happy hat would be too happy to accomplish the mission unless properly entrained, but then the tower would be of no danger to anyone wearing a happy hat."

"A happy hat? That's funny!"

"Yes, a happy hat. Can you keep something under your hat?"

"Sure."

"The fact that we hired you and that you and I are discussing your neighbor's suicide and the death tower is no coincidence. You have been chosen to market the happy hat."

"You're kidding me."

"No, I am not kidding. Think of it as the hidden part of your job description. Here, take this card. Call Madame Huong. Use the code name, 'General Peace'. She will brief you on what you are to do for us."

Tracey's Stuff

"May Tracey Flagler rest in peace," I said to myself, as I perused her anxious handwritten confession last evening while savoring several of Helene's scrumptious Palm Beach brownies:

"My connection to The Source is so amazing that I want it for others," Tracey wrote before she took flight to The Beyond. "They will believe it when they see it. A million dollars would help me to have the great stuff everyone wants and therefore to be their teacher. I have always wanted to be an example of the best of both worlds and to be proof that one can be happy and wildly successful and abundant in this one.

"I have always wanted stuff as a physical human, as proof that I have a connection to The Source, proof that my connection to The Source has value in the physical world, proof that the joy of being sourced can be easily translated into the stuff that brings physical security in this world. I want to feel my stuff, to have proof that I am really here and am really amazing. I have always wanted things to prove how amazing I am. I want to prove my ability to teach my amazingness. And of course I want stuff for my own fun and love and comfort. But I really don't believe stuff has value in itself. Stuff gets boring after a while. Everybody wants stuff. I want more than just stuff. Is success is based on physical stuff? No, the success is not in the stuff itself – success is based on enjoying and appreciating physical stuff."

George Berkeley certainly agrees with Tracey, that stuff has no value in itself. I happen to be a channel for George. He would like to discuss stuff in general on the Oprah Winfrey Show, and has asked me to manifest this brief interview:

WINFREY: George, I'm glad to have you on the show. I can tell from your handsome face – Oh my, what a divine aura it has – that you're not the stuffy philosopher I thought you might be.

GEORGE: Thank you, Madame Winfrey.

WINFREY: Just call me Oprah. By the way, I understand that you are a British Empiricist. Just what is an empiricist?

GEORGE: An empiricist believes that experience, especially of the senses, is the sole source of knowledge.

WINFREY: Okay, that makes sense, but your bio also says you're an idealist. How can a sensationalist be an idealist?

GEORGE: Sensations perceived are really ideas in the mind. Since all knowledge is of perception, only ideas are real, so the idealist is a realist.

WINFREY: Hmm. What about this chair, is it real?

GEORGE: Nope. But your perception of it is real, and that is an ideation.

WINFREY: Yeah. So I'm not an idiot to think the chair itself does not really exist because I'm an idealist?

GEORGE: Right.

WINFREY: What about spirits, do they exist?

GEORGE: Of course they do, but they cannot be perceived.

WINFREY: What do spirits do?

GEORGE: They mostly think. A spirit is a simple, undivided, active being, directly aware of its own existence, but we cannot see it.

WINFREY: Really?

GEORGE: Really. Spirits are really real. I am a spirit.

WINFREY: But I can see you.

GEORGE: What you see is really not my dear self.

WINFREY: I see. Now the folks at Yale say you are the first great American philosopher. I thought you were British.

GEORGE: I gave my farm in Rhode Island to Yale when I returned to London. I split my library between Yale and Harvard.

WINFREY: Good, good, that's good. So you were in America.

GEORGE: Right, for about three years. I came over with my dear wife, Ann Foster, with a plan to establish a seminary in Bermuda for the sons of colonists and American Indians. I obtained a charter for the college and some private grants, but Parliament didn't come up with major funding, so I had to call the whole thing off.

WINFREY: That's a shame. We can't depend on government funding. I just started a school for girls in Africa.

GEORGE: I know.

WINFREY: It's not easy. We've had troubles.

GEORGE: I know. There's always going to be a scandal. Evils always attend great goods – evil needs its contrary, good, to be evil. Take my word for it as a bishop: you are blessed in the eyes of the Lord for starting your school in Africa. In fact, although my ideal school failed to be manifested in Bermuda, it was my effort to establish it caused me to be recognized for my good intentions and to be consecrated a bishop.

WINFREY: Praise the Lord!

GEORGE: Yes, indeed, I second the emotion.

WINFREY: George, have you been following Paul Bowman's best-selling reflections on the late Tracey Flagler?

GEORGE: Yes I have. Paul is one of my channels. The poor girl put too much truck in stuff.

WINFREY: But every self-respecting girl has to have some stuff, right?

GEORGE: At least Tracey was in possession of the truth about stuff: that no matter what it might be, stuff has no value in itself; and if she had focused on that, she would not be in purgatory, figuratively speaking. Tracey wanted to have stuff to appreciate. She apparently believed stuff existed, and was not yet aware that careful reflection on the subject would have led her to the incontrovertible conclusion that the stuff she wanted did not really exist outside of her mind. What she longed for was the appreciation, not the stuff. I proved long ago that stuff in general is just an empty concept. There is no such thing as material substance in the world. If Tracey had been an immaterialist, you might have her on your show this afternoon instead of me, as I am a bit outdated.

WINFREY: Hmm. Immaterialist? That means matter does not exist?

GEORGE: If matter did exist, it would be of little moment. It's like the accountants say in accordance with one of their generally accepted principles: "It's immaterial." Meaning the so-called fact of the matter is inconsequential in itself.

WINFREY: Whoa. Please elaborate a little bit, so people won't think your knowledge is just foolish talk.

GEORGE: Well, a little talk is not enough to persuade most people that my proposition is not absurd on its face. Yet it is as plain as the nose on your face that, from your own perspective, when you think about it long enough, that neither the nose nor the face exists, but are simply reflections.

WINFREY: I can make out the tip of my nose, but....

GEORGE: It's not on your face but in your mind with your facial experience. The value of stuff perceived rests in the perceiver and not in the stuff.

WINFREY: Yeah, it's like, like, like beauty is in the mind of the beholder.

GEORGE: Yes it is. It all is. Perception is a judgment on sensation. I proved beyond a shadow of a doubt that the heat of a hot iron is not really in the iron.

WINFREY: Then why is it called a hot iron?

GEORGE: It is not a hot iron; it's a hot-feeling iron. The hotness is not in the iron. In fact, the iron itself is unknown, and, in my opinion, does not exist as an object. What Tracey perceived was not the objects she thought she needed in order for her to be recognized and approved of by others. She perceived the ideas she had about stuff, as if stuff existed, and her reflections on her perception, and what others thought they perceived, caused her to believe that stuff exists; yet it is really the perception and not the thing that existed for her.

WINFREY: Yeah, but "as if" is good enough for some people, and the appearance of having stuff and getting respect from others because one has it is a fact we must deal with, whether stuff is ultimately real or not. And there is some stuff like food and water that we can't do without no matter what it is or is not. What about my 2.5 billion dollars? Won't that buy plenty of stuff even if stuff doesn't exist?

GEORGE: Spoken like a liberal intellectual, Oprah. Money is an abstraction that facilitates the communication of ideas. The abstraction is not a thing in itself. And allow me to remind you that extension, figure, solidity, gravity, motion and rest are all habitual judgments on sensations, and do not inhere in material objects, but are directly perceived ideas; the objects themselves are not perceived. Sights, sounds, tastes, smells, and touches have no existence absent the mind.

WINFREY: Are you saying that sugar isn't sweet? That's odd.

GEORGE: Sugar is not sweet in itself, it simply tastes sweet; and the fact that it tastes differently to different people demonstrates that sweetness does not inhere in the sugar, nor, for that matter, does any taste whatsoever inhere in foodstuff. As for the primary qualities, if it be allowed that no idea nor anything like an idea can exist in an unperceiving substance, then surely it follows that no figure or mode of extension, which we can either perceive or imagine, or have any idea of, can be really inherent in matter, not to mention the peculiar difficulty there must be in conceiving a material substance, prior to and distinct from extension, to be the substratum of extension. Be the sensible quality what it....

WINFREY. Whoa, you're driving me batty already. I think I've got it, but I'm concerned that pressing a matter so contrary to common sense, that matter does not even exist, although that is the very subject we are talking about, might be talk about nothing, and might cause people to be suspicious about the most sacred and unquestionable things, such as the existence of God, and the reality of love.

GEORGE: I beg your pardon, Madame Winfrey. God certainly exists, and the world, which is really nothing but minds and ideas, would exist in God's mind even if we were not here to perceive it.

WINFREY: Would God then perceive the world as an ant or an elephant, or some other member of the animal kingdom?

GEORGE: As a godly human, first of all.

WINFREY: Great.

GEORGE: We must remember that our receptive minds are passive; therefore mind is not the cause of its ideas. Since no objects exist hence objects do not produce ideas, there must be willing spirits that produce them. The divine mind is one mind over many minds, and when those minds are turned away from the mire we call stuff, towards the divine mind, they are bathed in the light of love, and it is then and only then that the soul may experience the joy of The Source Tracey Flagler longed for.

WINFREY: We'll be right back. We'll be right back. Stay tuned.

Tracey's Whales & Oprah Winfrey

In 1969, long before South Beach became the super-chic living end that it is today, a red-nosed and stubble-bearded alcoholic at the cockroach-invested and flea-ridden Colony Hotel told me that the decrepit southern end of Miami Beach inhabited mostly by poor old Jewish folk was "the end of the world. There's nowhere to go when you're really down and out, sonny," he said, pointing at the ocean, "but out there, to drown."

I didn't give suicide much thought at the time, as I had more pressing concerns. I barely had the bare necessities of life paid for that month. I sold a pint of blood for starters. I scraped dried-up banana peels off the deck of a ship, and then I worked for a while loading trucks at bankruptcy auctions. My success was assured when I was hired as the night clerk at the Pennsylvania Hotel, where I was given lodging in the freight elevator housing on the roof. I lived on breakfast specials, and half-rotten fruit and vegetables I bought at discount at the market, and saved half of my pay every week, inserting a twenty-dollar bill in every ten pages of a Bible I found in the lobby. I didn't read scripture that much, but I did preoccupy my spare time reading Russian novels, as well as my favorite book during storms, Moby Dick, so the guests gave me the benefit of the doubt and called me "rabbi."

As a matter of fact, I was not religious at all; my father was a non-practicing Jew; my stepmother, a fundamentalist Christian, tried to make a Christian of me before I ran away from home, but to no avail.

I felt that the Christians I encountered at her church were phonies: they kept telling me that their Jesus loved me, and I knew from their behavior that they did not, so what good was their Jesus to me?

As my good luck would have it, a pot-smoking Jewish American Princess who had been ditched on the train down South by her sugar daddy wound up in my lap one night. I followed her back to New York. The affair did not last long as my presence interfered with her career as a porn star, so I used the balance of my savings to fly to Waikiki, where I went broke and got a job with a hotel tycoon in the nick of time. He didn't pay me much, but he taught me a major secret of success: if you walked up to ten girls on Kalakaua Avenue and asked them to bed, one of them, on the average, would say yes, so don't get upset if you get slapped in the face until then.

Little did I know that I would return to South Florida just before Hurricane Frances and the Dalai Lama landed, or that an Internet chat-room friend, an ex-Navy SEAL whose Internet handle was 'Doc', would rescue me from the storm and take me to the Clay Hotel, Al Capone's old gambling hideout on South Beach. Speaking of the Mob, my one-legged friend Doc, may he rest in peace, told me interesting stories about hanging out as a kid with Meyer Lansky and company – his mom had married one of Lansky's sons.

South Miami Beach had changed considerably in my absence. The poor man's paradise had been gentrified by a new sort of vulgar people, the nouveau gentry. The cost of living was high, and the low-paying jobs that served the high-livers were not easy to get unless one spoke both Spanish and English. I found myself going broke, which would have been a damn shame for a man my age in this money-grubbing Age of Greed, especially if he didn't smoke crack and drink and stumble along Washington Avenue swearing like a sailor at the top of his lungs. His predicament is certainly not our fault – he's obviously mentally ill and has refused to go into rehab and take legitimate drugs.

Shame has always given self-titled noblemen like myself due cause for suicide, hence I proudly confess that, after my recent return to South Beach, the fear of becoming homeless where homelessness is now so despicable caused me to consider drowning myself off the beach at the end of Lincoln Road, where there is no lifeguard station. Of course few people take pride in self-murder nowadays, so I would make sure to pick a red-flagged riptide day, and sneak into the water wearing swimming trunks in order to make my drowning look like an accident. At least my children would not be further disgraced by the fact I was their estranged father. Besides, I still had an accidental death insurance policy, for which the premiums were duly deducted every quarter from my meager checking account; therefore they would have the death benefit to boot, which might posthumously boost their opinion of me.

Lady Luck came to the rescue yet again. Or, as Oprah Winfrey would have it, I was graced and blessed by the divine source, The Source that is not necessarily religious, if I understand her rightly, because regular religion is not that popular among the growing numbers of New Age fans, who are looking forward to the advent of a brand new kind of Christ presaged by such prophets as formerly homeless Neale Donald Walsch, who reinvented God in his seminal series, Conversations With God.

Now Neale Donald Walsch's self-dialogues are of particular interest to me because Tracey Flagler, my sweet next door neighbor, who idolized Oprah Winfrey, was possessed by Conversations and related New Age culture before she sacrificed her life to the gods in South Beach. Mr. Walsch was apparently spoiled by unusually permissive and loving parents, and his would-be omnipotent god or child within was victimized by the world he encountered, the hated Western World with its pompous religion, higher authorities, rights and wrongs, shalls and shall nots. He was thoroughly pissed off – four failed marriages and unsatisfying relations with his children aggravated him all the more – so he went on the homeless path and angrily addressed his god along the way, noting well his god's answers. He won the wrestling match, and emerged with best-selling books instead of a pronounced limp. Nietzscheism had of course forgiven him and his readers in advance; or rather there was nothing to forgive since right and wrong are wrong ideas to begin with. Every victim of Western civilization can find temporary relief in Conversations with God.

The intelligentsia refrain from openly guffawing at popular discourse lest they lose their politically correct status. Intelligent fascists used to chuckle privately when Hitler promised something for everyone, except the Either/Or Jews – hate-based group-love needs a new scapegoat: the West will do. Muslims may take a big bow soon: they are in effect frustrated Jews who need to protest their religion and become postmodernists. Postmodernism tolerates all cultures except the traditional hierarchical culture of the West, which has given untold millions of Judeo-Christians cause to suffer needlessly. Nazism, with its return to pagan spiritualism and barbaric natural religion, is tolerated or embraced despite its right-wing authoritarian tendency, a big-corporation tendency with which the hated capitalist West has a presiding affinity – leftist ideologues perhaps correctly noted that fascism is the perfection of capitalism.

Mr. Walsch is professedly a writer, editor, and public relations man by trade. Ten years before he went on his road tour with his god, he called himself Neale Marshall-Walsch and served as public relations professional for such New Age figures as Terry Cole-Whittaker, minister for the New Age Church of Religious Science. Suffice it to say that the New Age is nothing new to him – or to anyone for that matter, for it is in fact a reversion, or regression, if you prefer, despite the progressive claims. However that might be, his god made numerous contradictory statements to him from within during his homelessness sojourn without – he profited handsomely on his dialogues with his permissive superego after they were published, even the more so after Oprah said Conversations with God was one of her favorite books.

For instance, Mr. Walsch asked his god if suicide is wrong. An evasive answer was spit up to him from within; that is, from the subjective realm beyond relative good and evil: “The question cannot be answered to your satisfaction, because the question itself contains two false concepts; it is based on two false assumptions; it contains two errors. His first false assumption is that there is such a thing as "right" and "wrong." The second false assumption is that killing is possible. Your question itself, therefore, disintegrates the moment it is dissected. ‘Right’ and ‘wrong’ are philosophical polarities in a human value system which have nothing to do with ultimate reality—a point which I have made repeatedly throughout this dialogue. They are, furthermore, not even constant constructs within your own system, but rather, values which keep shifting from time to time.”

Furthermore, his god told him that, although “death does not exist,” death is “always a gift” and “You are the cause of your own death. This is always true, no matter where, or how, you die,” that is to say that “you cannot die against your will.”

Well, then, it would appear that every death is in fact a suicide, dying is merely an act for drama’s sake on this stage we call the world, and suicide is therefore a pretense and perhaps a complete farce at that.

However comforting that might be to enlightened people, I had seen corpses and I had experienced grief hence I was somewhat anxious over the possibility of my own non-existent death by my own hand. Instead of going for a fatal swim one early morning as planned, I decided to surrender to whatever might happen. My cowardice was rewarded with a call from La Mujer de Oro de Coral Gables, Florida – she had a temporary job for me counting other people’s money, paying two-and-one-half times what I had been asking for.

I counted my blessings. It was as if I had been saved from the abyss by Moby Dick, the great white whale, and had been spit up on land from the depths of despair to scour the beach for ambergris yet to be happy enough with a few empty shells or sea-shekels.

Not that I praised the Lord or rushed off to a temple convinced of the existence of that Negatively Existent One alluded to by the Tetragrammaton. The great white fish, I speculated, had always been my mystical temple, the nuclear-powered Nautilus that conveyed me from shore leave to shore leave, just as the mosque is the great white camel that carries the Muslim across the barren desert, and just as the great white elephant carries the Hindu god through the demonic forest.

I don't know why, but despite my salvation I used my spare time to compose biting diatribes against the very society that was feeding me. One bitter tome, on permanent, either-or truth, I entitled 'Doom is Nigh Again'. Since something within me is merciful, I have a compassionate sequel in mind, on relative truths, which I shall entitle 'Doom Indefinitely Postponed Again'.

How could I be so ambivalent? How could I be such a hypocrite as to curse the octopus that feeds me, and even go so far as to curse the All Mighty?

Excuse me, my confusion is causing me to sink into a trance: "Never mind, don't feel guilty," I hear Neale Donald Walsch's god saying, "You will join Hitler in heaven." "What say you? Hitler in heaven? But Hitler was dead wrong!" "Hitler did nothing wrong," responds the postmodern neo-pagan god. "Hitler simply did what he did, although he thought he was doing the right thing." "That's what all right-wingers say when they do wrong, that they are doing the right thing." "I have said time and time again that there is no right and wrong in the universe." "But Hitler was still a monster!" "Your opinion that Hitler is a monster is based on the fact that he ordered the killings of millions of people, but as I have said, millions thought he was right, and death does not exist, anyway. Hitler didn't hurt anyone. In a sense, he didn't inflict suffering, he ended it."

"Nonsense! Death must exist if millions were killed. My family on my father's mother's side was murdered in the camps." "Let me tell you," declares the neo-barbarian god, "that what you call death is the greatest thing that could happen to anyone, for at the moment of your death you will realize the greatest freedom, the greatest peace, the greatest joy, and the greatest love you have ever known." "Will numerous blond and blue-eyed virgins with large breasts and big thighs be waiting for me in an icy wonderland?" "But of course." "Then let my god tell you this – the name of your god is god spelled backwards!" "Not!" "My god is better than your asinine, ass-sniffing dog." "My god is not a dog! Oprah Winfrey recommends my god, and her people said she didn't air the two-hour interview with me because the people are not ready for my advanced perspective on the advent of our charismatic New Age Christ., who will unify the world one day." "Oprah's audience is not ready for another Hitler yet, that's why she turned you down – she's not stupid, she's read Tolstoy, she's an intellectual." "You must read my Conversations with God."

"My god is better than your god," I heard my voice singing, "my god is better than your god, my god is better than your god, my god is better than your god...."

Egads! Excuse me. Where was I? Yes, ambivalence. Spit up by the whale. Like Jonah, I suppose, to preach doom. They say Jonah is a minor prophet. Sophisticated rabbis have said that he didn't want to preach doom at Nineveh as the Lord had commanded, because he figured the Lord would make a fool of him yet again by forgiving the repenting heathen and sparing Nineveh, just as Jerusalem had allegedly been spared despite Jonah's prophecy of its destruction, wherefore Jonah's reputation as a "true prophet," gained by the fulfillment of his prophecy in the time of Jeroboam II, would be fully ruined, for true prophecy comes true at least half the time if not always.

So the rabbis said that Jonah fled from the prospect of being shamed by the Lord he so adored. He hired a ship and took to sea, but when the vessel was confronted by the Lord's apparent wrath, in the form of a storm, Jonah asked the sailors to throw him overboard that they might be saved from his Hebrew nemesis. They did so and were converted to faith in the one-god when the sea was immediately becalmed. Jonah was swallowed by the fish, and contemplated the grandeur of the Lord from his submarine, longing to be once again in the Holy Temple, but he had never left it, and the whale of a fish spewed him up on land again, where the command was once again given, to prophecy disaster to the wicked inhabitants of Nineveh.

But Jonah was angered, and I think not because the Lord had made a fool of him for prophesying a false outcome, as many teachers would have us believe, but because the Lord was merciful and did not bring disaster down upon the heads of the wicked. Good Grief! When, after all, will justice finally be done? When will the wicked get exactly what they deserve? When will "I'm sorry" not be good enough? When will Justice tire of one repentance after another, which enables the wicked to sin again and again? I think the text makes Jonah's motive plain:

"This, O Lord, is what I feared when I was in my own country, and to forestall it I tried to escape to Tarshish: I knew that thou art a god gracious and compassionate, long-suffering and ever constant, and always willing to repent of the disaster. And now, Lord, take my life: I should be better dead than alive."

I think Jonah had had enough of mercy and forgiveness. But that is just my opinion: I am not licensed to practice religion and my opinion is not intended to be spiritual advice; for that one should consult a bona fide spiritual master.

Oprah Winfrey is perceived as the high priestess of the postmodern relativity religion. Young women, especially those who believe there is something wrong with them, that they are weird or freakish, women such as my late neighbor Stacey Flagler, hang on her every word as gospel. Her veracity is proven by her wealth. Her endorsement of books such as Conversations of God sends sales through the roof.

Almost every liberal-minded person loves Oprah Winfrey, and Yours Truly would love to be on her show and have her endorse this living novel in progress. I would raise myself to the full height of my mediocrity and say something to please everyone regardless of their characteristics, so that everyone might enjoy the cake I had baked for them. Then I would lower the Doom boom.

WINFREY: Walter, are we all equal or not?

DAVIDSON: Everybody is equal no matter what.

WINFREY: Right.

DAVIDSON: I mean equal under our law.

WINFREY: OK, the courts should not discriminate against us because we are rich or poor, gay or straight, or because of our colors, looks and faiths, right?

DAVIDSON: Right. And there is a titanic struggle going on between good and evil on at the highest level, and justice will be done below.

WINFREY: Good and evil, hmmm. That is what your purchase-on-demand book, *Doom is Nigh Again,* was all about, right? It didn't sell so well?

DAVIDSON: Yeah, yeah, it was a failure, I sold only twenty-nine copies, to friends and acquaintances, and gave another twenty copies away, to reviewers, and I sent along a copy to your people. I maintained that true faith is faith in justice, faith that it shall be done some day no matter what, although nobody knows exactly when, and on that day everybody will be accounted for by a valid statistical methodology. Evildoers on balance would be doomed once and for all.

WINFREY: Uh-huh, but then you thought justice would be too hard on too many people, you believed they needed to be forgiven and loved, so you changed your mind?

DAVIDSON. Yeah, so I wrote *Doom is Postponed Indefinitely*.

WINFREY: It's a blessed book, a best seller.

DAVIDSON: Thank you. I am so delighted that you recommended it. But sometimes I have my doubts about its relative truths, and wish the prophecy of a lasting doom mentioned in my first book would come true, because then prophecy would be so alarming that people would really repent, if there were anyone left to do so. I think there are too many false prophets among us today.

WINFREY: Oh, no, Walter. We have had enough dooms all ready, don't you think. I think everyone got the point. Where did you get that idea, anyway?

DAVIDSON: From the *Book of Jonah* and Herman Melville's *Moby Dick*.

WINFREY: I saw the movie. The whale got away. The black whales got killed and cut up. And I remember Jonah warned people, and they were sorry, and they got away.

DAVIDSON: Melville had a thing about whiteness, about its purity, but he wasn't prejudiced. I think Jonah got mad at God because God forgave them instead of making an example of them.

WINFREY: OK, we have a commercial coming up, and before that I want to....

DAVIDSON: Ope, I think if you read Moby Dick all the way through, you would highly recommend it. May I read something quickly from this copy I brought you?

WINFREY: Well, uh, thank you, but this is not on the....

DAVIDSON: Please, Ope, please?

WINFREY: OK. Be quick.

DAVIDSON: "Jonah did the Almighty's bidding. And what was that, shipmates? To preach the Truth to the face of Falsehood! That was it! This, shipmates, this is that other lesson; and woe to that pilot of the living God who slights it. Woe to him whom this world charms away from Gospel's duty! Woe to him who seeks to pour oil upon the waters when God had brewed them into a gale. Woe to him who seeks to please rather than to appall! Woe to him whose good name is more to him than goodness! Woe to him who, in this world, courts not dishonor! Woe to him who would not be true, even though to be false were salvation! Yea, woe to him who, as the great Pilot Paul has it, while preaching to others is himself a castaway!"

WINFREY: Wow! OK, when we come back, we will find out why Paris Hilton abandoned her career, gave her fortune away to charity and took vows of poverty.

Tracey's Inadequate South Beach Brownies

Tracey Flagler, duly inspired by her favorite star, Oprah Winfrey, reached for the stars, and now she is gone, we know not whence, perhaps to become a star herself. I caught my first glimpse of the young woman out of my bathroom window over my bathtub two years ago as she was chaining her bike to the railing of the outside staircase that runs up to her apartment. She was a tallish, relative attractive, fit brunette of thirty, with a withdrawn, spiritual sort of demeanor. When my next door neighbor Lawrence moved out, she cleaned out his apartment for the landlord because she was in arrears on her rent. She wanted Lawrence's big bed, so she knocked on my door to ask me to help her move it. We hauled her lumpy mattress into the alley, and then lugged Lawrence's heavy Sealy mattress and platform down my building's flight of steps and up hers. I had a coughing fit, and nearly fainted from the exercise, so I joined a gym the next week with good results. She promised to bake me a batch of brownies for helping her out.

Tracey's studio was packed tightly even before the installation of the big bed. She had a huge stuffed chair and an enormous couch; hence the only running room left was for her big, fluffy cats, Ginger, Pepper, and Splenda. They tore about the place from the top of one thing to another when I entered carrying one end of the bed, and then settled down on high to stare at me. The scene reminded me of the movie, Bell, Book and Candle.

Since the day I helped Tracey install the bed, I glanced into her front windows whenever I showered. She eventually got herself a cheap but beautiful pole lamp with yellow, green, blue and red shades around its bulbs. A few days later it appeared by the dumpster out back, smashed to smithereens. I encountered Tracey in the yard, and I mentioned that I once had had a lamp just like it, when I lived in downtown Kansas City. She said her kitties had knocked it down, and that my brownies were finally ready – she was sorry for the delay, she said, but had been working double shifts at the restaurant.

The brownies were not that bad nor were they very good. I had already been spoiled by my friend Helene's Palm Beach brownies. She lived down the street, and she often gave me coconut macaroons and brownies out of the large batches she made. Her macaroons were much too salty, but the brownies were truly scrumptious. Helene feels enormously inadequate no matter what she does, so I did not mention the salt. Like many other women of her age conditioned by Twiggy-consciousness, she thinks she is too fat, when in fact jogging like crazy and boxing a few times a week offsets the sweets. Indeed, her curvaceous body gave me occasion to virtually drool from time to time. One evening she remarked on her fatness. As if my desire were not insulting to her Victorian sense of propriety, I said that slightly voluptuous women turned me on. She yelled at me, insisting that I had called her fat, the very thought of which might cause her to panic and revert to the anorexic way of life. She ordered me out of her apartment, saying she could never trust me again. I went slack and exited with a bag of brownies in my hand.

I knocked on Tracey's door the next day and gave her a half-dozen of Helene's brownies. I would not have done so if I had known that she was even more plagued by feelings of inadequacy than Helene. While rummaging through Tracey's stuff after she passed away several months later, I came across this entry haphazardly scrawled in one of her confessional notebooks:

"Walter gave me some of his girlfriend's brownies this morning. I tried one and was utterly humiliated. Her brownies are so much better, much richer than mine, I said. He was nice – he lied and said they weren't better, just different. But they were better, a lot better, that I know and won't lie about it, because nobody will see this so I don't have to lie. I just cannot excel in anything I do. I've been crying all night. The brownies brought me back to this thing that something is wrong with me, that I don't have what it takes to be successful, that I'm only happy with simple things, that I'm weird and slow and inadequate, so inadequate that I hate myself, and I wish I were dead, but (illegible) bring myself (illegible) because I'm too inadequate to....

"I have known joy, and I don't want it all to be just about feeling joy. I want to do great things, like make great brownies and do stuff, to have real stuff, real people and real, lasting situations, but I feel bad about everything I feel like a bad daughter, a bad girlfriend, a bad person. All I wanted to do was to be normal, to have some fun, to relax, to fit in. I want to believe that I'm brilliant, and that even my weirdness is part of my brilliance. I want to believe that that I can handle anything, to make really great things, to be a leader. But I hate being on the leading edge, being (illegible)....

"What is it all about? I know it is supposed to be all about joy, all for joy, so I want to know joy in human form and in forms that help me focus and feel and live as part of humanity, but (illegible)...(expletive) inadequate.

"It seems stupid that we are eternal beings, and that it goes on forever and ever and we are not supposed to get it wrong yet we never get it done right – why do anything then? I want to be an eternal being born a human being, have those beings complement one another, and not feel that one cancels out the other or makes it inadequate, or feel that I am only one of them. I would like to find my balance in these things, and to have (illegible)....

"No one taught me this crap as a kid, taught me why I'm the one who is weird and why the others are normal. It pisses me off that I'm the one who feels weird, that I cannot even make great brownies like normal girls do! If I died this week what would have been the point? What would my purpose have been? I feel so uneasy, so anxious all the time, I feel (illegible) the inadequacy is (illegible) I feel so (illegible) my (expletive) brownies are inadequate like me...."

It occurred to me that ambivalent Tracey might have better chosen Martha Stewart as her model than Oprah Winfrey, at least for the sake of making scrumptious brownies. In terms of knowing joy and having fun, so-called hash brownies used to do the trick for those of us on the leading edge, the cultural avant-garde of the sexy Sixties – we were the sex buds of our era. The secret to making dynamite brownies was to bake the buds at a very low temperature for a few hours to bring out the oils before chopping the buds up and adding them to the brownie mix.

Oh, those were the good old days when everybody of note was supplied by the not-so-secret source, the legendary Pusher Man. A Vedic hymn of the ancient Hindus called him Soma, a god in his own right as well the plant and the drug extracted from it. Whosoever partook had the power to fly beyond the limits of heaven and earth, and felt strong enough to pick up the Earth and carry it about wherever he wanted. We sincerely believed life was supposed to be fun, that we were entirely free to create separate realities and to be and do anything we so desired. Indeed, forty-five minutes after we swallowed our soma, we did not feel we should have to do much more than think of something for it to become, lo and behold, materialized.

It was as if we were omnipotent, immortal gods in those days, especially when we were higher than kites. Of course we had been naturally spoiled by our permissive upbringing, and believed that all we had to do was ask in order to receive, just as the world's greatest magician had advised two thousand years ago. Good intentions were good enough for us. Heck, we thought the whole purpose of life was to have joy and to be joyful. Joy is that wonderful feeling of unmitigated freedom that allows one to love oneself everlastingly in the infinitesimal Now, to live in the Now without impedance from without, to live harmoniously without interference from any other point along the infinite line that circled back to each and every one of us. After all, how could points interfere with one another and still be points? For if they touched they would overlap, and then there would be only be one point; wherefore the entire universe would be collapsed at that point.

Forsooth there was seemingly nothing without to restrain us in those paradisiacal days, for we lived in harmony; we felt free to be free with our feelings as our guide, and individuals differed only in the quality of their emotions. If a body did not feel good, if it stood in the way of joy, it was a merely a rag to be tossed aside painlessly with the help of an overdose, for the assumption of another form at will.

Our era was a pipe-dream that went up in smoke. Our joy was short-lived. We copped out and got steady jobs working for the Man. Many of us just said no to the drugs that made us feel so powerful. Withdrawal from our version of mass delusion is still a bit painful, we may never fully recover, but we do not feel very inadequate, for we had a great deal of fun in our moment of fame, and the most of us survived the joyful rite of passage. Besides, we are getting old now; the pangs of inadequacy are felt more keenly by those who believe they might live forever and fear the boredom of failure forever will drive them mad.

Love is no longer free. Money is the power-drug today, more potent even than the sex that may be purchased with it. The oldest profession is a noble undertaking in South Beach: the prostituted look is in. According to the latest survey by the Miami New Times, a struggling fashion model might charge $500 for a single night, or rent herself out as a girlfriend for $12,000 month until she achieves fame and fortune. Money will supposedly buy anything including heaven. War not peace is the watchword. The competitive war of all against all is the universal religion. The winners are rich and famous, and most liked are those who started out in rags. After all, what makes America great besides its military might is that a few poor people have a chance of getting filthy rich, an incentive that keeps everyone contributing to the gross national product instead of beheading the winners. Oprah Winfrey is a great person because she was once poor and is now worth over $2.5 billion – she has an extraordinary gift of gab, but most people could care less how she got her fortune, and that must make her a little sad at times.

Of course the dream of greatness is nothing new; it began on that prehistoric day when someone stood on their two hind legs and pointed at the stars. Every life would endure forever if it could hence life craves power in one form or another. Great powers are greatly appreciated by all who crave power, who would be loved by the whole universe and therefore would be irresistible. We naturally feel inadequate when we behold the great models worshipped by society. It is no wonder that people feel inadequate when confronted with by the celebrated stars they both love and hate.

"What is greatness?" Tracey asked herself in a little note. "I am seeking greatness through the alignment of my desire with my belief. Who are great people? Famous people, because they are rewarded by society for what they offer. Greatness is when I am a famous person. I feel like something is wrong with me. I hate that. I hate being alive. I want to be alive but it sucks to be alive. I hate it that I'm not famous. I hate alcohol and drugs. I hate this culture that bases fun on what I have. I hate Abraham. I wish I was dead and I wish he was dead so I could stop loving him. I'm trying to tap into true love and the humans that have it. I know in my heart that I'm so great. Have I had fun here? Do I want to be here?"

That she did not want to be here became all too obvious to me when I found her remains. I knew something was wrong when a waitress from the restaurant where she worked showed up and banged on her door three days in a row, pleading with her to come out and go to work, but to no avail. I grew increasingly worried by her friend's anxious pleadings. She said Tracey had not come to work nor had she called in. I told her that I had not seen Tracey at all. It was unlike Tracey not to go to the beach in the morning and do yoga, ride her bike in the afternoon, and go to work in the evening. Her blinds were pulled day and night, although there was a light on within, which was highly unusual. And I had not seen that handsome brown fellow come by for some time – I gleaned from her diary that he was the "source" named Abraham, the fellow who apparently had shared "the secret of the universe" with her. I climbed her steps and banged on the door one fateful morning – nothing. One of her windows was unlocked. I pushed it up, called her name again and again, and then climbed in the window.

And now I have my regrets. I wish I had not frustrated her with Helene's Palm Beach brownies. If only I had known about Tracey's secrets, about her connection to the source, about the book she was writing, I would have done my utmost to befriend her, and by my example prove that nothing exists and is perfect. But such was not preordained. My remorse is assuaged, however, by the fortune I found in her apartment, a fortune worth far more than the million dollars she wanted to buy her freedom with. Certain metaphysicians have consoled us with the doctrine of metempsychosis – it is best not to die while eating a ham sandwich lest one return in the form of a pig. Perhaps Tracey's soul will transmigrate to a higher form. Perhaps we shall meet on the Oprah show once I have cashed in, in which case I shall hand her a million dollars with my best wishes.

Tracey's Happy Holiday

This is the season to be jolly, but I am sad at present, and I look forward to saying good riddance to this two thousand and seventh year of the Common Era, or, if you prefer, the same year of the Lord Jesus Christ. Of course this year had its good side: there is no evil unattended by some good, and vice versa. The Dualists say Good shall overcome Evil in the end, and then and only then shall there be one god, an entirely good god at that, but until then we shall have them both. I am thankful for a goodly number of reasons, which I am in no mood to presently enumerate, and may the New Year be a happier one for us all. But for now I am sorrowful.

I have just received word that Nathan, scheduled to be home for Christmas, was killed in Iraq. His grieving grandfather, a minister and a missionary, had tried to persuade him not to go to war; but he was an idealistic youth: he wanted to exercise the patriotic ideal handed down to him from high authority; he wanted to "do the right thing" urged by the president of the United States in the name of the unseen father higher than his father, whosoever that unknown all-mighty might be. Of course we support our troops, but I for one envision the devil dangling by the neck at the end of a flag from a pole while his councilors face a firing squad below.

The year did not begin well for my family: my niece's dad went into the backyard and shot himself to death with a rifle shortly before she turned sweet sixteen, apparently over economic woes. They were close; we could only imagine the sorrow and horror she felt – she did not show it. My aging father, always solicitous for her welfare, was left extraordinarily distraught. He had already suffered from an Orpheus Complex for nearly seventy years: my mother died of polio, shortly after I was born, in her twenty-first year, and since then he often wept over several poems he had composed in commemoration and then frequently rewrote throughout his life, changing a word here and there, but never getting them quite right. He finally joined her shortly after his ninetieth birthday – how such a wide difference in age is resolved in the hereafter no one knows, for sure, except perhaps the psychic who swears that all persons there are thirty years old regardless of their age at time of death.

And then my friend Doc gave me his old, slider cell phone for good luck. I received a call on it a few weeks later, from his new number, but it was not him: it was his son, who informed me that Doc had died. If there is a life similar to this one after death, with money and all that it implies, I shall buy him that cheeseburger, as I had promised to do in order to break his insistence on paying for our greasy meals when we got together. And now the nation's elders have sacrificed young Nathan's life, needlessly, in my opinion, if it were not for the need of the young to imitate their elders and prove their mettle. Doc understood all that: he proved himself several times over in Vietnam, and elsewhere on Black Ops; he was a warrior by profession, loyal to his nation and its commander-in-chief, no matter who he might be.

"Woe is me," is certainly unsuitable in my case. It is not as if my entire family and many friends besides were killed collateral to the struggle for so-called liberty. Again, I have due cause to be thankful for many things, not to mention just being alive in the first place and the chance to rejoice once in a while as my own end appears over the horizon. Still I have been morbid as of late, and even the more so since I found the beautiful body of Stacey Flagler, the girl next door, decomposing in her apartment. Her diaries revealed that all she wanted out of life was fun and joy and love, which amounted to the same thing.

"Joy," she wrote, "is the whole point of life."

The hodgepodge pop-culture endorsed by her frantic idol Oprah Winfrey had convinced her that the purpose of life is personal joy, that death is really a myth, that good and evil are relative, that even Hitler went to heaven because he thought he was doing the right thing, that there is really no such thing as death, that we are all immortals who choose and discard one body or another and take up yet another at will, so she discarded hers, and I found it rotting in her studio.

Unsurprisingly, she had taken up democratic - everyone can now sit down and hold séances with their ids, alter egos, superegos, and other psychic entities if need be, and become mediums for ghosts, spirits, souls, and gods and the like. I supposed that was all a lot of nonsense; but then again, wishful thinking along with the fact that our culture, hoping for a better life, worships death somewhat more than life, has given me cause to dabble in the occult, and, in this living novel, to dwell at length on the incidentals of the demise of one Stacey Flagler, may she rest in peace if she's not dancing for joy in paradise.

The pop-culture of today is constituted by warmed-up leftovers of the postmodern dishes we relished in the Sixties. We said yes to the occult long before we just said no to hallucinogenic substances that helped us to get together, get with it, freak out and enjoy the vibes. Our vibes back then are today's vibrations.

And now the mesmerizing high priestess of the Virtual Church of O has endorsed something called the Law of Attraction. Someone used to refer to the Power of Magnetic Thinking. We don't need to hold on to an iron rod dipped in water to cure our woes nowadays. We can plug ourselves in to the will-power-source within, direct the current to our internal generators; the amplified flow, oscillating according to our fondest dreams, may create magnetic fields capable of attracting whatever we might want, or at least set up an aura of the right wavelengths to attract money and mates like bugs, if not send some sort of electromagnetic ray to reel in the prey from afar, or perhaps radio-waves emitted by our Diamond Crystal Radio implants might enable us to use the fabled Power of Suggestion on people at a great distance.

But it is difficult to keep up with the amazing progress of science, so analogies drawn from that field to create useful science fiction aids to successful thinking might be exposed as faulty, which would cause people to look like fools and to lose faith, It's best to keep the scheme and the technical methodology in which one has faith secret, lest the critics, who would naturally resent one's luxurious lifestyle were it obtained, do everything they can to retard the novitiate's progress. We used to speak of a person's magnetic power quite often until someone familiar with magnets pointed out that like does not attract like, as the ancients thought; in fact, as many married couples know very well, opposites attract, wherefore it would seem that praying for wealth might attract poverty.

Maybe it would be best to take vows of poverty in order to be loved by the universe and to therefore gain catholic fame and fortune. We may recall that the wise old Jew in Balzac's *Skin of Chagrin* renounced things and pursued philosophy: things flew to him as if he were a magnet; he got what he did not want, namely everything, including an antique store wherein the wild ass's skin was deposited until the suicidal fool who had given up philosophy took it as a gift.

For all we know, the holes vacated by electrons in the Jewel in the Lotus race around in a direction contrary to that of the electrons, as the electrons vacate and fill hole after hole. And who says that space itself is negative, when we may think of it as positive; the things that fill it negate it, hence are negative. Let it be positively negative if you prefer. The negative has its positive attractions after all, especially in a liberal consumer democracy, where the motto might well be "Find a hole and fill it ad infinitum." The miserable shall be comforted and the meek shall inherit the earth. We are all bums at the bottom of our being: we should have more faith in Nothing.

My positive might be your negative and vice versa. Debit and credit do not mean minus and plus, but mean right and left; and then there's the question, to whose right and left? But never mind scientific skepticism; positivism gets sensational results, so let's be positive and embrace positivism. It is generally accepted that we must be positive to obtain a fortune including an attractive, sexy mate. That's the ticket to winning friends and influencing people profitably. Think negatively and suffer the consequences accordingly: live in poverty alone or with a broken-down old nag or an abusive, beer-guzzling football fan. I am feeling more positive now that I think of it. Let people be miserable if they want to be, and then maybe someone will come to comfort them, but don't depend on it in our grasping society, where so many people have only Jesus for a friend.

Yes, I am getting into a better mood at this place in our living novel. I feel like crawling completely out of the disheartening dumps I've been in. I've turned off the television and have picked up Stacey Flagler's notebooks. Although she finally negated herself, there is something very positive about the way she felt. If she had kept the faith for another year or so, I believe she might have lived her dream, perhaps even be blessed and graced by the likes of Oprah Winfrey.

"I have faith in the Law of Attraction," Tracey had written large on a page in a brown spiral notebook, "and I make myself the focus of my energy field. I have a sense of connection to it no matter what or where I am. I need to be a vibrational match to be wealthy and to attract a true mate. I would experience the joy I am seeking if I were involved with someone who is somewhere within my vibrational range. I need to feel good, and know that there is enough security, connection, and stability.

"Getting stuff and mates is not about getting what you deserve. Fame and success is not about talent –it is about the alignment of vibrations. Nothing is about getting anything – it is all about vibration.

I shall be a vibrational match to whatever I want, and attract it right to me. I shall pretend that my vibrations attract a wealthy mate and that he matches my vibrations and buys me an amazing home. I shall focus connecting energetically to what I want and receiving it. The more people caught in my web the better, as long as I put myself first.

"Abraham says just get happy and all things will flow into my experience. The universe loves me; the only thing I have to do for the universe is be as happy as I can be: that is the trade and the exchange, I feel swept away into a current because it feels good to connect to the energy stream. It is fun to be in the freaking energy stream! I want the energy connection. Oh, magic is afoot! I feel such excitement about the thoughts I'm thinking! It's all about my imagination as reality. Imagination is the great launching pad! "I feel money flowing now. I feel myself being in the top 5% financially. What is it that I love so much about money? I love it for the flow of energy and stuff that it makes possible, for being able to buy things that help to make it the energy flow, to put out great vibrations that attract people who love me. Some man is going to get a great girlfriend who loves sex, who knows how to have fun and focus on the best, on the most excellent things, on sensual and spiritual things.

"I love the name of the book I am writing about this stuff, Intentional Genius. What a marvelous title! I feel my energy flowing in that project. I feel I am on the brink of success! My vibrations will attract wealthy geniuses from all over the universe. And I love doing channeling too, relaxing and lowering my vibrations so my mind can be the medium for Abraham, Immanuel, Seth and the others. I do love my own energy so much, the energy flowing from myself, in pulses that say 'love, love, love, love.'

There you go. I am feeling cheerful now, so I shall give Stacey's memory the benefit of the doubt. She might be immortal after all. Happy Holiday, Stacey, wherever you are! We love you!

Pseudepigraphic Oprah-Krishna Interview

The evidence of birth is made more public than that of death; we see many more babies than we do corpses during our lifetimes. Medieval people made no bones about the public display of bones, for instance celebrating All Saints Day in ossuaries, but we moderns manage to keep the most obvious fact of death more or less private, hidden away in hospitals, morgues, funeral homes and cemeteries. Although I was not familiar with my neighbor Stacey Flagler, when I discovered her beautiful body decaying on her bed on Thanksgiving Day, lying there as if it were an offering to the gods of this world, I was profoundly affected.

I worked as a hospital orderly in my late teens, and I saw and handled several dead bodies during the course of my duties – I noticed that deaths came in bunches, shifting from one wing to another. Making money seemed to be the purpose of human life, so when I counted the pittance I received as pay, which was less than a dollar an hour, I told myself that I had better hurry up and become a millionaire before it was too late. But I was really in no hurry, and I soon forgot the corpses I had seen, for I believed in my heart that my own life would go on forever one way or another, that I had all the time in the world to do anything I wanted to. Now that I am well over the hill, so to speak, and feel myself slowing down and going to pot; now that my contemporaries, friends, and family members are dying off; now that my bank account is short by nearly a million dollars; - I confess that I have serious doubts about my perpetuity.

Indeed, I am moved to admit that my body will undoubtedly perish. As for my soul, I do not know what that might be other than the "I" that I refer to as mine, the elusive unity or apperception and phantom pilot of the ghost within my machine, a selfish mental field that will most likely perish along with its platform. The thought that my self is merely software, the notion that I am an epiphenomenal ghost that did not exist in the first place, is comforting when not appalling. If I were never born, then how could I ever die? Still the machine does not want to run down, wherefore I cling to this self-conscious life in between nothing and nothing.

Stacey Flagler let go of hers. She had a terrifying craving she could not satisfy, an inability to relax due to an insufferable energy impelling her frantically forward at all costs. Witness this small portion of her handwritten confession to Abraham, the psychic entity that she adopted from Esther Hicks and then channeled for her own consumption:

"I feel like I have never translated my desires into a recognizable life that others could identify with. And why do I want that? So I can relax. Then I would feel like I had succeeded. Success would make me relax, because that would be my joy, and I want to be an example of joy, to teach joy. If only I could relax and let joy and passion and well-being in. But if I relax and find relief, then I don't believe anything will have meaning! I might as well not have a body. I want to have a specific meaning in this minute, and what I want that specific meaning to be something I asked for and created. I want to know that I am powerful and can create security while I'm here, security for me, Tracey, the human being. As I look back I have always been looking for security even though it doesn't seem like it, the security of easy joy and of more and more joy. It has all been about finding and keeping joy, choosing love, and love choosing me. Nothing is wrong with me – I've actually been attempting for seven or eight years to create my own reality and to accomplish that on a certain scale would be the ultimate security. At the same time, I've always wondered if something was wrong with me, if I should abandon my search for joy, to give up my commitment to stability in a physical sense. I think that creating my own reality puts me at a disadvantage. I believe I am unsure of it because just being happy, focused on love, having fun, and feeling contented will not inspire me to be that productive. I work harder discontented. So what does security feel like? It feels like I have to change external things to be secure, so to be secure I have to be insecure, to move from insecurity to security. To be secure I have to focus on my personal preferences, focus on things that matter to me. What do I want security to feel like? What matters to me? Non-resistance, keeping my body and mind clear of resistance, being in a state of joyful grace. Having physical things to focus on here can bring me joy. But then I will transform into something non-physical, and so why do any of this at all? Why does any of this matter? I am to fulfill my reason for being by just being here and being on the leading edge and having my personal preferences, but how do I get in on it?

What is it that I wish to experience in the meantime, until I am fulfilled? I want the relaxation and joy that allows me to focus. Why? What is the point of anything? Do I really believe the point of life is to focus on and obtain my personal preferences? Yes, I do, but I just don't know what they are anymore, or if I can even handle what I've asked for, or why they continue to included alcohol and drugs when that is clearly self-destructive! I just want to connect, but then you say that I need to be so connected that they are irrelevant to my connection, and then I can feel the greatest joy. You say I can find that connection on my own. But I think I need a partner to relax. I feel I must have a reason to love, someone else to love besides myself, and then my problems would be solved. But I know from what you say, Abraham, that what I am really longing for is the connection to Source, to my inner being. But if I am looking for my source, which I had in the first place, then why did I come here to look for it? Why have these circumstances with all of the fear and worry and insecurity that goes along with them? What is the point, then? It just doesn't make sense! "I want to love someone who loves me back in the same way and it is mutual and they see that potential too and they hold onto that potential."

She had turned to the popular postmodern culture for advice, to the splendiferous effusions of Oprah Winfrey; to the contradictory conversations of Neale Donald Walsch with his super-egotistical god; to the pronouncements of Abraham channeled by Esther Hicks; to the big Secret that must be kept in order to be believed in instead of laughed at – small secrets are leaked from time to time to the tune of hundreds of millions of dollars. She was told that the purpose of life is to have joy, that death is just a myth, that everyone can create their own planets in a universe that loves them. Since she did not feel the joy and love, since the reality she wanted to create was not obtained at will, and since life had no specific meaning for her, she chose the myth, perchance to be incarnated on another planet if not reincarnated on this one.

The risks attending such a fatal leap are mortal indeed, and I was duly mortified by Stacey's premature departure. She took too big of a chance, I thought; that is, I thought so until she contacted me from the so-called "Beyond" the other day, from that place referred to at funerals as the Better Place – more on that later. I thought she might not have taken her last life if she had fallen into the right hands. Not that I blamed Oprah, the new high priestess of the New Age, or the postmodern gurus she or her guest celebrities endorse, nor did I blame their crowd of sympathetic sycophants, for elevating Stacey's expectations and then letting her down when she reached out to them and discovered they were too busy creating their own realities to attend to her desperate needs.

We like to believe that our social icons are really special, but we should realize that, in order to attract the average person and be orthodox and politically correct enough to be popular, one has to specialize in mediocrity to a certain extent. Attractive models are not famous for their brains but for the looks or power or money we would like to have. That is not to say that every model is superficial, or that the spiritual world is really deeper than the supposedly shallow material world. Stacey was confused by the supposed relationship of the spiritual and material; she thought she needed stuff or the million dollars to buy it in order to make matter and spirit one and the same; then she would supposedly be completely relaxed, well-loved and joyful, but she preferred the spiritual over the material, and to that extent she was not on the wrong track, she just needed a better model to keep her train on the right track to joyful love and eternal bliss.

To that end, I mused after Stacey's early end, Bhakti Yoga would have been a much better vehicle for her than the claptrap jalopies haphazardly slapped together from Sixties' New Age leftovers. She was right: There was nothing wrong with her, at least not for wanting the security and joy of loving and being loved. Untold millions of people are spiritually dissatisfied: there is nothing abnormal about that. Stacey might have been able to tolerate and even love the world with herself in it this world if only Krishna had appeared on the Oprah show, as in the unauthorized depiction below, and Oprah had plugged the Bhagavad-Gita. The wheel has been turning for eons; it is a terrible waste of time trying to reinvent it.

Stacey would have loved Krishna, I opined, so much so that she might have blissfully devoted her every action to the Supreme Personality without consideration of worldly reward. Chanting Hare Krishna, singing praises, dancing and cooking delicious food would be fun. Krishna is playful, by the way, so she would have had some of the fun she yearned for. And she would not have to worry about piling up a bunch of stuff to be happy. On the other hand, loving obedience to authority might not be her cup of tea, although some of that would be useful on a part-time basis. She loved and hated the same men, was conflicted over her objective relationships: she wanted but at the same time rejected love objects. She had to continually tell herself how much she appreciated the little things of life, and I doubted if the big things she thought would gain her respect from others would be good enough for her. In fact, no particular thing or person seemed to be good enough for her. She wanted to be connected to the source of everything, to be at-one with the infinite, yet it is extremely difficult to love an abstraction. Wherefore I imagined a synthesis of Bhakti Yoga, or love yoga, and Raja Yoga, or mystical yoga, would have suited her best; she might do both at the same time. Karma Yoga, or productive work yoga, was out of the question, for she really did not want to work for things, and Jnana Yoga, or philosophical yoga, would probably have flown over her head, for she wanted to get to the point.

OPRAH INTERVIEW WITH LORD KRISHNA

OPRAH: Glad to have you on the show, Krishna.

KRISHNA: The pleasure is all mine, Oprah.

OPRAH: I have been reading about your pastimes. I see you made the National Inquirer again, just last week.

KRISHNA: Don't believe every scandal you read. I like to have good, clean fun.

OPRAH: Clean fun? What do you mean?

KRISHNA: I always take plenty of soap with me.

OPRAH WINFREY: I understand that you like diary maids.

KRISHNA: I love them with my flute.

OPRAH: And you slay demons.

KRISHNA: That's what they say.

OPRAH: How many lovers do you have?

KRISHNA: Billions if you count my many forms.

OPRAH: Wow! And you love them all back? How can you serve and be faithful to them all?

KRISNA: I can be everywhere at the same time.

OPRAH: It's like television broadcasting?

KRISHNA: Sort of.

OPRAH: I feel blessed and graced with so many eyes on me, so many people adoring me. How do you feel?

KRISHNA: Transcendental.

OPRAH: Is that a feeling?

KRISHNA: It is your bliss if you are my devotee.

OPRAH: Bliss? Do people love you for the joy of it?

KRISHNA: Many of them do, especially my bhakti people.

OPRAH: And what is bhakti?

KRISHNA: Loving devotional service.

OPRAH: Why bhakti?

KRISHNA: Bhakti softens the heart and removes jealousy, hatred, lust, anger, egoism, pride and arrogance. It infuses joy, divine ecstasy, bliss, peace and knowledge. All cares, worries and anxieties, fears, mental torments and tribulations entirely vanish. The devotee is freed from the grinding wheel, the cycle of births and deaths. He attains the immortal abode of everlasting peace, bliss and knowledge. The ultimate goal of bhakti yoga is to obtain a feeling of pure bliss.

OPRAH: Oh, yeah. Joy is the key word, right? People devoted to you feel splendiferous, feel blessed and graced all the time, true? I mean they feel really good about themselves, experience a lot of joy.

KRISHNA: Well, yes, all of that and more, but that kind of joy is just the beginning. Bliss is the ultimate state, and is far better than what you call joy.

OPRAH: But isn't bliss joy?

KRISHNA: By bliss I mean something similar to what some of your Stoic gurus called apathy.

OPRAH: Oh, no, that doesn't sound good. It sounds depressing.

KRISHNA: Bliss is actually an indifferent feeling. It transcends good and evil feelings. My devotee is ultimately free from joy and depression and the dread of harm. She expects nothing. She is pure, just, impartial, devoid of fear, and could care less about profiting from the results of her action. She is most dear to me and to others, for she is not afraid of them nor are they afraid of her. She who does not rejoice, find fault, complain, or covet stuff, who is not interested in good and evil results, is most worthy of my love.

OPRAH: OK. I guess. Is there equality?

KRISNA: My beloved servant is equal-minded to friend or foe, the same in honor and dishonor, in cold and heat, in pain and pleasure. She is satisfied with whatever happens: she not anxious about what might or might not happen in future. Praise and blame are the same as far as she is concerned. She pretty much keeps her mouth shut because she is content and therefore does not have to talk much. She is blissful everywhere, and may be what you call homeless, for she does not need to live in the same place all the time. I am her home. Her heart, full of devotion to me, is secured by me.

OPRAH: But she must get mad sometimes.

KRISHNA: Of course. But again, my devotee who is free from enmity, well-disposed towards all creatures, merciful, wholly exempt from pride and selfishness, the same in pain and pleasure, patient of wrongs, contented, constantly devout, self-governed, firm in resolves, and whose mind and heart are fixed on me alone, is dearest to me.

OPRAH: Okay, but is she immortal?

KRISHNA: This religion as I explain it is the sacred ambrosia, the very religion of immortality. Those who come to me full of faith, intent on me above all others, and united to me by devotion, are my most beloved.

OPRAH: But what about people who don't want to bow down to a personal god, don't believe in things they can see, and think stuff is vulgar. What about those who can't stand the thought of a definite god and want to love the unbounded and infinite being, the unseen?

KRISHNA: There are many ways to skin a cat.

OPRAH: Please. I love cats.

KRISHNA: I spoke figuratively so that your audience might better understand me. There are several ways to the same goal. Those who worship me as a person, with constant zeal, with the highest faith and minds placed on me as a person, are held in high esteem by me. But those who, with minds equal toward everything, with senses and organs restrained, and rejoicing in the good of all creatures, meditate on the inexhaustible, immovable, highest, incorruptible, difficult to contemplate, invisible, omnipresent, unthinkable, the witness, indemonstrable, shall also come unto me. Yet mind you that for those whose hearts are fixed on the unmanifested, the labor is greater because the path which is not manifest is with difficulty attained by corporeal beings. But for those who worship me, renouncing in me all their actions, regarding me as the supreme goal and meditating on me alone, if their thoughts are turned to me, O Oprah, I presently become the savior from this ocean of incarnations and death. Place, then, your heart on me, penetrate me with thy understanding, and you will undoubtedly dwell hereafter in me. But if you should be unable at once steadfastly to fix your heart and mind on me, strive then, O Oprah, to find me by constant practice in devotion. If after constant practice, you are still unable, follow me by actions performed for me; for by doing works for me you will attain perfection. But if you are unequal even to this, then, being self-restrained, place all thy works, failures and successes alike, on me, abandoning in me the fruit of every action.

OPRAH: That is a mouthful. Can you sum it up for us?

KRISHNA: Sure. There is something for everyone or nothing if they prefer. There are four ways to supreme unity. The ways of knowledge, practice, meditation; and renunciation. Knowledge is better than constant practice, meditation is superior to knowledge, loving renunciation of the fruit of action to meditation; final emancipation immediately results from such renunciation.

OPRAH: You mean to have stuff is bad? Can you have sex? What about drugs?

KRISHNA: You can have nothing but the clothes on your back, a bowl of rice and a flower, and you may also have scrumptious vegetarian feasts for me, but take no drugs, and you can study and dance and chant all day, and have sex at night, but only for procreation of more devotees, and you can do lots of other devotional acts as well. On the other hand, you can meditate a lot, be driven around your ashram every day by a different beautiful woman or handsome man in a different Rolls Royce, and you can have a little laughing gas during your dental appointments, if you like. Just say no to drug use in general, including alcohol and tobacco and marijuana, without a special prescription from me, and don't allow your disciples to traffic in drugs even if they don't use them. Worshipping me is the greatest natural high of all.

OPRAH: So I can keep my $2.5 billion?

KRISHNA: As long as you devote yourself to my service, you will be immortal and blissful regardless of your wealth – remember, the Lord Himself is Opulent, and he loves the poor. Whatever is rendered to me is returned with compound interest, or, if you want less, then you will get less, and if you have faith in nothing because nothing is perfect and permanent, then nothing shall be yours for the asking, but it's best to ask for nothing at all because nothing is infinite and nothing really works. Remember, it doesn't matter what you have or do in my favor, for all things are mine and should be devoted to me anyway. When you are mine, when you love me, the universe loves you back and is yours no matter what you have on hand at the time of devotion.

OPRAH: I think I like the loving yoga you mentioned best. How do you do that?

KRISHNA: Here, I brought you some anklets. Please put them on. And here's a bracelet with some bangles.

OPRAH: Oh, thank you! They're beautiful. Listen to the little bells tinkle when I shake a leg! And the bangles, here, how they jangle so wonderfully. Very exotic!

KRISHNA: Yes, please stand up and shake a leg with me. Take this tambourine and jiggle it in the air. Good. Now take my hand. Let's do some hip hop dancing and chanting. Repeat after me, Hare Krishna, Krishna Krishna, Hare Hare. Hare Rama, Rama Rama, Hare Hare. Got it?

OPRAH: I wish Ellen were here. Okay, here we go...Hare Krishna, Hare Krishna.... I feel blessed and graced. I think I love you Krishna.

KRISHNA: The feeling is mutual. Here's a pouch full of my books, and you will find some flowers on top. You can carry it over your shoulder. My favorite book is the Bhagavad Gita.

OPRAH: Then I shall recommend it to everyone! Oh, this is fun! Hare Krishna, Krishna Krishna..... We'll be right back after this commercial....

The Spiderweb

Tracey Flagler flew the coop, whether to heaven or hell or to nothing at all nobody alive really knows for sure, although wishful people lie about such things or about nothing at all. If we are to believe her diaries, Tracey was seldom satisfied with whatever she had on Earth.

"I am so deeply disappointed. The gap between what I have and what I believe and desire is so big that I wish I were dead so I could feel relief. I want to experience myself as a powerful creator so I can have whatever I want, so I can just fulfill myself with what I am seeking here, with joy, joy, and more joy! All I want to have is fun, and that and only that is the true meaning of life. But if I look back on my life I see there has been a lot of joy but I always thought it would lead to something provable or recognized by society and that would make me matter, make me valuable. If I listen to Abraham, I do matter, because just by my being here I move the universe forward."

Tracey obviously did not want to enjoy joy all by her lonesome self: she wanted to be recognized by others, which would, according to her diary, require obtaining a great deal of stuff to impress them with. And of course she wanted to be loved unconditionally; that is, loved for her substantial self regardless of her qualities, which were attractive to men indeed: she was, as we already know, the stand-in for Charlize Theron, a movie star declared by Esquire Magazine to be the sexiest woman alive, and Tracey would have been that star herself but for a twist of fate.

A fellow named Abraham is frequently mentioned in Tracey's notes, someone she met at a concert in San Francisco while filming Sweet November. If her diary is a faithful record of the truth, she enjoyed many nights with him, although there is nothing explicitly sexual to be found within.

Abraham taught her that life is supposed to be fun because her natural self is joy. He taught her that she could be, do, and have anything she wanted, create her very own reality by simply imagining it so the universe could reflect it right back at her. The universe, he said, adored her, and knew her intentions, and in fact moved according to those intentions. If only she would relax into her natural state, all would be well for her, and she would live in her unique path of joy, a path of everlasting life paved with money and bliss. And, since her self was everlasting joy, and since she had chosen the body she inhabited, it stood to reason that she could discard her present body painlessly, without being sick at all, and choose another one at will.

No man is good enough for idealistic women. She listened to Abraham and did her best to have faith in his line, but the stuff she wanted did not appear forthwith, and she wound up hating him so much she wished him dead along beside herself, because he kept telling her it was her fault for not creating the world she said she wanted, making her feel guilty look like the bad one instead of the victim:

"I hate what has happened and mostly I hate it because I look like the bad one, as if I screwed up, like he is my victim instead of me his victim. I just want to scream at him and choke him and say to him before he strangles, If you co-created this with me, you asshole, I want to just leave and find a new boyfriend, but dammit, I want that same feeling I had with your presence, so I am angry at all men, and that anger makes me feel powerful, makes me feel better than feeling powerless. I have had all of your self-created universe that I can stand, and I wish you were DEAD and I were DEAD!"

The more I delved into Tracey's anguished soliloquies, the more I began to think that Abraham was an imaginary lover, a figment of her flighty imagination, especially when he was mentioned in context of other planets in other galaxies. "Is it possible to be brainwashed by aliens?" I speculated. Women and men are not from different planets, but that is not to say that we are not visited by aliens. Fools may take figures of speech too seriously, but the fact of the matter is this: men are not from Venus and women are not from Mars, nor are Earth feminine and Sky masculine. Men and women are in fact from the same planet although not determined by the same element. The essential male ascended on all fours from the mud, while the essential female descended from the air. In fine, men evolved from some sort of thick and flat mud-fish that developed legs and arms, and emerged from the slime to plod along in the muck, while women slithered lizard-like from the water. They grew long back legs to run from the brutes; their front flippers, vestiges of amphibian life, turned into the wings of the tiny dinosaurs that took flight. The flying-dragon girls were so frightened by a colossal hurricane that they panicked and returned to Earth, where some became discombobulated chickens, and others found large, web-footed lagoon creatures stuck in the mud to cling to. One lagoon ape was good as another but none were good enough for them. Wherefore humankind evolved. Women's hips and breasts eventually grew so large from childbearing that they could no longer take flight no matter how much they wanted to. Physiognomy still accounts for their flighty disposition. Witness the vestige of their airy origin, the bird-like features of their bony arms and shoulders.

Real men know very well that women are flighty. For instance, a middle-aged, paunchy man sporting a gold Rolex watch at Starbucks on Lincoln Road shook his head as his wife flew out of the door. He turned to me and said, "She's flying off to shop; she doesn't need the coffee to fly. Women are flighty, you know." "Oh?" I responded. "Haven't you noticed? I love women, but women are plumb crazy by nature." He had a point, I thought, thinking of my friend Helene: she was blown out of her nest at the Waldorf; or rather she was beaten out of it by a rich and powerful con man who looks like a horned and hairy toad and who consorts with duplicitous neocons. She landed in South Beach, a hedonist's resort, where she cannot relax long enough to get laid, and I can't say that I blame her, knowing what she's been through at the muddied hands of muddled men in general. The slightest mention of sex on my part gives her cause to panic and go into hysterics. She would like a "generous" and "passionate" beast to cling to, but no man is good enough for her, particularly if his passion is between his legs. I'm afraid that in a moment of desperation she might just say yes at random and wind up with the Creature from the Black Lagoon – at least Dr. Frankenstein's monster would really love her. She has taken up with lesbians since she loves power and lesbians have plenty of it on South Beach. Not that there is anything wrong with lesbianism, which might be one of God's plans for humankind: it is said that the Y chromosome was once as large as the X chromosome, but the Y has greatly diminished over the millennia, and in 150,000 years will vanish. Given the right mutation, such as that had by a certain kind of lizard, all human beings will be females. Like those lizards, humans will still have to stimulate one another to procreate parthenogenetically, hence one might suppose that everyone will have a greatly enlarged clitoris. Of course Helene, who is at heart an old-fashioned woman, would find this sort of science-fictional speculation repulsive, but boys will be boys and bring toads home from time to time.

But better evidence can be had from a celebrity than from a nobody like your present author. Oriana Fallaci, during a 1967 interview with Dean Martin, asked: "You respect men more than women, don't you?"

"Oh, yeah! I mean, I also have some women friends. Ursula Andress, for instance, and Shirley MacLaine and Barbara Rush.... But apart from these ladies, I'm more relaxed with men... 'cause men are down-to-earth and more honest, and I can get a repartee with them, have fun. Women instead are crazy, crazy, crazy, and they're flighty, and they are always looking for somethin', and they always tell you how good they are."

Oriana Fallaci's 'Sixteen Surprising Interviews' with famous people are happily collected in a book entitled The Egotists, published by Henry Regnery Company. It is certainly must reading by all those who think they might find the secret of becoming rich and famous and powerful in such books. Of course they will notice that the secret changes with the fashions. One constant is that gods and great men are usually forgiven for their crimes, or may even be admired for them. And the works of gods and heroes allow for great mysteries; for instance, how boxing is not violent and how stabbing your wife in the belly can be a crime but not a violent act:

"The knife in my wife's belly was a crime," admitted the late Norman Mailer to Oriana Fallaci. "It was a grave crime, but it had nothing to do with violence. As for the fights, well, boxing is not violence. It's a conversation...." You see, a boxer is a noble artist who transforms violence into something beautiful. A violent person picks fights, starts fights.

"Nor can I remember ever having hit a woman – a strange woman I mean. I may have hit a wife, but that's different. If you are married, you have two choices: either you beat your wife, or you don't.... I like to marry women whom I can beat once in a while, and who fight back. All my wives have been very good fighters."

Sean Connery, the representative he-man of his time, was asked to name three men and three women whom he admired. Nikita Krushchev, Stanley Matthews, and Pablo Picasso were the males he picked. As for women, he could not think of single woman he admired, although he liked women a lot. "A character like me, who loves life and appetite and strength, can't get away from sexual desires. And so, when he stops to assess a woman, he can never make out where that things finishes and pure admiration beings."

No doubt Tracey Flagler, if she were still with us, would be happy to know that the Duchess of Alba, reputedly one of the richest women in the world, did not even know how many rooms her palace had, or how many millions her art masterpieces were worth, nor could she have cared less about the value of her jewels:

"I do have a few jewels, the family jewels. But I don't know what they're worth, I really couldn't tell you. I never bothered about it. Oh, all this talk about money. I find it disgusting, hateful. I hate money, I never bother about money. What use is money, so long as you have enough to live well? The necessities. What's the use of having more?"

Tracey did not know the Duchess, but she made this little note in her diary: "What if I can just talk and feel myself into joy without a lot of stuff to prove how valuable I am? Is that enough? What if I am joyful but I just live a simple life, pay my bills and live in my beautiful little South Beach studio, to not worry about anything, like I've already retired, or that I am a noble woman with just enough stuff. But when I think like that I feel I have failed, because I need a mission in life and somebody to do it with to feel more connected. Why, really? To have fun, that's why, instead of being pulled into other people's stupid visions, which are fine for them, but not for me, but I am pulled into the vortex anyway, pulled by my selfish intentions, and at bottom all my hopes and dreams are ground down to nothing, there is nothing but nothing, I can't find anything to hold on to, I just want to be dead unless I can have that eternal perfect moment, that joy and fun promised by Abraham. Now I am so angry. I HATE this whole situation. I feel weird, hopeless and stupid. I intellectually understand what Abraham says, but I don't understand emotionally. No matter what I have, no matter how much I appreciate it, just enough stuff to live on is just not enough, I cannot lead a simple life. Abraham promised me JOY. He lies like them all. I HATE Abraham, I HATE me. I HATE all you con men! I HATE you!"

Tracey might also be please to read that Geraldine Chaplin's dad thought that a girl of twenty should support herself, and so did she, so she rented a room in a basement, went flat broke, didn't ask her parents for anything, and then, "Luck came to my rescue," she told Oriama Fallaci. "I happened to meet a photographer friend." He invited her to a shoot, "and in those four days I earned no less than two hundred thousand francs."

Now that was a fabulous sum in the early Sixties. What was two hundred thousand franks worth, then, in terms of today's depreciating dollars? Was it the Name that rescued her, or was it Charley Chaplin providing funds behind the scenes? Or was it that fickle lady of fortune, Lady Luck?

Oprah Winfrey would no doubt say that poor Geraldine Chaplin was graced by the divine albeit not necessarily religious source. "Why then, was not Tracey Flagler thus graced? Is not Flagler a famous name? Was not her father rich?" I asked a crab spider as I took a shower and gazed out the bathroom window into the window of her former apartment across the way. It is now occupied by a Haitian. He sits or lies on the floor when he is at home – he has no furniture, which he could easily get for nothing from South Beach alleys, where a couple of hundred vagrants stretch out on discarded chairs and couches from time to time.

The crab spiders are truly amazing. They are triangular creatures with humped red backs and horns on the edges. Their flat underbellies look like white faces with black eyes. The rapidity with which they can elaborate symmetrical webs between palm tree leaves and buildings is truly astonishing – I have knocked down some that that got in the pathways, only to discover them rebuilt a few hours later. Sometimes I gaze into one of the faces suspended in the air and ask a question, such as, how come Tracey Flagler did not get rich and famous? Tracey Flagler, who was suspected of being a witch by her downstairs neighbor, spun many webs in her notebooks, in the form of spoked wheels, the spokes expressing related desires emanating from an affirmative "I" in the hub.

"I feel satisfied with my place in the now and my place in eternity," affirmed the "I" around the hub at the center of one wheel. "Spoke 1. I do believe what Seth and Abe & Emmanuel say about being eager. Spoke 2. I would like them to just do it for me. Spoke 3. It is not that I don't want to exist eternally; it's just that I want to enjoy what I have now, not worry about the eternity in the moment. Spoke 4. The universe wants fun for me, for me to be secure in joy and to have stability just because it feels good. Spoke 5. I like living the best of both worlds, enjoying my now and maintaining what matters to me. Spoke 6. I love seeing my internal joy outwardly manifested in a cool home, $ $ $ and freedom and abundance etc. Spoke 7. I can focus on whatever I want to focus and bring it to me. Spoke 8. I believe that the universe responds to my focus and matches my expectations. Spoke 9. I do believe that being is eternal, that being is enough & that I will exist eternally."

We might believe that Tracey was just spinning her magic wheels, and that great expectations, planted in her by false prophets who would have been stoned to death in Jeremiah's day if the law had been dutifully enforced, led to her depressing demise by her own hand. But we of little faith might be wrong. Perhaps her only fault was her feminine flightiness; or rather in the fact that she flew her coop altogether instead of expanding on it as the little spiders outside her door do. If only Tracey had stuck around, built a larger web and stayed poised in its center, lots of juicy things might have come along in due time. Durability might have been the key to her success.

"Durability means something that lasts because it wants to last, not because it is built to last," Mary Hemingway told Oriana Fallaci. "A scrap of iron exposed to the wind and the rain and the sun is not durable because it needs no effort to be so. But a spider's web is durable. It looks so frail, but it resists the fiercest storms and winds and rains....

In the garden of our house in Cuba there were always lots of spiders' webs, and one obviously thinks they'll be swept away by every storm. Tropical storms are ruthless in their violence, they destroy trees and roads and houses. But they don't destroy spiders' webs. Spiders' webs wave in the wind, letting the rain drops through the mesh, and when the storm is over one always finds them in the same place, practically untouched."

Mary Hemingway spoke truly. Our flighty little birds in South Beach get killed off by the hundreds in our storms, but our spiders and their webs stay put. That is, unless one deliberately knocks them down with a broom handle. And then they bounce right back. May Tracey Flagler bounce right back from the netherworld, if there is such a place, and, if not, may someone else do so in her place. Now that would be an enduring epic story worthy of Oprah Winfrey's endorsement, and not the ephemeral journalism, broadcasting, propaganda and film writing that Ernest Hemingway thought it best for a great author not to waste his time on.

We love you! We love you!

Epitaph

Rest in Peace

www.ingramcontent.com/pod-product-compliance
Lightning Source LLC
LaVergne TN
LVHW041039150826
845672LV00001B/383